PARTY GAMES!

BY MICHAEL MCMANUS

Published by Playdead Press 2024

© Michael McManus 2024

Michael McManus has asserted his rights under the Copyright, Design and Patents Act, 1988, to be identified as the author of this work.

A CIP catalogue record for this book is available from the British Library.

ISBN 978-1-915533-25-8

Caution

Playdead Press

www.playdeadpress.com

For Fraser and Sinéad

Party Games had its first production at the Yvonne Arnaud Theatre, Guildford, opening on 2 May 2024, followed by a UK tour through May-June 2024.

CANDICE	Krissi Bohn
LUKE	Jason Callender
JOHN	Matthew Cottle
ANNE	Natalie Dunne
SETH	Ryan Early
CHIEF WHIP, REID	William Oxborrow
LISA	Debra Stephenson
PRE-RECORDED VOICES	Sir Robert Buckland, Carolyn Quinn Simon Stallard

DIRECTOR	Joanna Read
DESIGNER	Francis O'Connor
LIGHTING DESIGN	Chris Davey
SOUND DESIGN	Beth Duke
ASSISTANT DIRECTOR	Haiqing Liang
MARKETING & PR	Sally Anne Lowe for the Yvonne Arnaud
PRESS	Amanda Malpass
VENUES LIAISON	Natalie Yalden, Tandem Marketing

A note from the Playwright:

This is my fifth play. It is also my first commissioned play and the first not to have its premiere production at the White Bear Theatre in Kennington, produced and promoted by me. I owe so much to that venue and to its kind and generous founding father, Michael Kingsbury. So many careers begin in the varied world of Off West End theatre and that wonderful, diverse sector deserves all the support it can get as it continues its determined recovery from the Covid-19 pandemic, lockdowns and the cost-of-living crisis.

The basic, founding idea for this play, was to weave a comedy out of the spiralling growth in influence and power of unelected advisers. This has been touched on elsewhere, of course, notably in "The Thick of It" on BBC Television, but, to the best of my knowledge, no one else who has personally been in "the room where it happens", has ever tried to bring to the stage the dangerous folly of this current direction of travel. Even within my own working lifetime, political appointees used to be kept firmly in their proper place by a resolute, even assertive, civil service. This is apparently no longer the case. The upper echelons of the civil service have been diluted and demoralised, in particular around the functions of press and media, by an increasingly blatant use of political patronage. After five years of Con-Lib coalition between 2010-2015, I can confidently say all the major parties are complicit in this.

When I took this idea to Joanna Read in November 2021, it amounted to no more than a few notes sketched out on a train journey, on the back of the script for my previous effort, "Maggie & Ted", which had recently enjoyed a successful run at the Yvonne Arnaud, directed by her. She asked what the scrawl was about, I told her and she asked "would it help if I commissioned it?" My answer was immediate and affirmative. There followed a testing writing process, across more than two years, with constant rewrites required, not only to improve the quality of the piece and hone the comedy, but also to keep up with some extraordinary developments in the real world of politics, in which this play is firmly rooted. Prime Ministers, Chancellors and lettuces came and went, but nothing seemed to improve for the mass of citizens. I soon decided this piece could only be an all-out comedy: not quite a farce (can any billing strike more profound terror into the heart of even the most dogged and resolute theatregoer than "a new farce"?) and certainly not a satire (it is too deeply rooted in truth for that and, anyway, we inhabit an age that satirises itself to destruction) but a comedy, contemporary, vivid, just about credible, proudly *sui generis*.

As we moved into the final 12 months of the Parliament elected in December 2019, what struck me forcibly, was the discernible lack of enthusiasm across the nation for any of the "mainstream" parties: Conservative prospects (already thin) jeopardised by the rise of Reform UK, while the Greens, particularly but not exclusively amongst younger voters, threaten to siphon off much-needed support from the Lib-Lab parties of the centre left. As a recalcitrant centrist myself, I opted in the play for what seemed to me an optimistic, if unlikely, prospect: the rise not of yet another extremist, rabble-rousing populist party of the left or right, stoking the fires of popular discontent for its own seedy purposes, but a kind of *rassemblement* of the civilised centre, under the leadership of an unlikely duo, one a woman drawn from Labour ranks, the other a former Tory, former minister and former MP for somewhere in Oxfordshire, who may or may not have attended a certain school. That latter character has been there from the outset, at the heart of the piece: the entitled yet insecure public figure, who craves adulation and laughter, who needs to be loved, who *loves* to be loved. He has many names in the real world, but we all know and recognise him.

That is how "Party Games" was born: ultimately a cocktail of Marlowe's *Doctor Faustus* and the Faust legend, edgy modern comedy, first-hand political insight, social observation and an attempt to capture some of the (rightly, in my view) growing public misgivings about the rapid, unregulated development of Artificial Intelligence. At one stage, the chief of staff, Seth Dickens, was going to break the "fourth wall", the one character empowered to address the audience directly, in a series of soliloquies, all in iambic pentameter. That ended up on the cutting-room floor. None of the characters in the play (truly) is intended to hew very closely to anyone in real life, but the piece does contain references to real political figures, rooting John, Anne, Seth and the others in a reality close to our own – an alternative future perhaps. Although my PM John Waggner is assuredly *not* anyone real or actual, he does, I hope, embody the relentlessly performative (and manipulatively comical) style of our most electorally effective contemporary public figures. He's just freed from the creaking party system that seems, once again, perhaps more than ever before, more a barrier to needed reform than a potential vehicle for it. Above all, in these troubled times, this latest age of anxiety, we have all sought to create something genuinely enjoyable.

It took five table reads to get us to this point, including one in spring 2023 that was decidedly "make or break" for the prospects of the play. Numerous superb actors have earned my thanks for playing a significant part in landing us safely ashore, including Clare Bloomer, Jilly Bond, Lisa Bowerman, Robert Daws, Ian Hallard, Oli Higginson, Lewis Jenkins, Joseph Potter, Dee Sadler, Simon Stallard, Abigail Thaw and Gary Tushaw. My thanks go to all of them, plus Elliot at Playdead Press and Ken Pyne for his lovely cartoons. I would like to give my thanks also to other friends who have supported me on this journey, including Fiona Adams Jones, Joe Boyle, Nica Burns, Joanna Carr, Fiona Lockley, Nicholas Robinson, The Real Candice, Barry Stewart, the team at Savages and my good friend and fellow West Ham sufferer Fraser Massey, to whom the play is jointly and affectionately dedicated. Above all, my thanks go to Joanna Read, who took a massive punt on me by commissioning the piece in the first place. I hope it proves to have been worthwhile for everyone involved.

Michael McManus

Michael McManus | Playwright

Michael has worked in and around the world of Westminster politics for his entire adult life, as a special adviser, parliamentary candidate, campaigner and national journalist. All that considerable professional and life experience now informs his playwriting.

Michael's first play, "An Honourable Man", which foresaw the rise of a populist leader in the UK after Brexit, had two sell-out runs at the White Bear Theatre in London in 2018. His third play, "The Trial of Donald Wolfit", became the second production to open in all of London after the initial spring/summer lockdown of 2020, again at the White Bear. His fourth play, the one-act "A Certain Term", has had two successful runs at the White Bear, in 2022 and 2023, as part of a double bill entitled "Generation Games".

His most successful play to date is "Maggie & Ted – On Air", which has proved to be remarkably durable despite the intervention of the Covid-19 pandemic: a sold-out, week-long trial run at the White Bear Theatre in October 2019 (attended, amongst others, by Lord and Lady Heseltine, Lord Hunt of Wirral, Baroness Bottomley, Michael Cockerell, James Naughtie, Lord Baker of Dorking, Richard Wilson and Lord Dobbs of "House of Cards" fame) was followed by two triumphant nights at the Garrick Theatre in London's West End at the end of the lockdown period in 2021 and a successful week-long run at the Yvonne Arnaud Guildford in October 2021. A new, fully-staged version of the play will enjoy its first production in 2025, marking the centenary of the birth of Margaret Thatcher.

Michael is currently working on a number of new projects for theatre, including a new musical featuring the songs of Marc Almond and Soft Cell. He also continues to write for national media, notably "Gramophone" magazine.

Michael is an actor too, represented by Savages Personal Management (www.savagespm.co.uk).

SCENE 1
DAY 1 (General Election Thursday)
9.59PM – A ROOM

JOHN alone then LX shows Luke and Anne, all watching TVs out front.

MISHA:	It's 10pm. Voting has ended in the general election and our exclusive joint exit poll from Opsi Mopsi and Who, Me, Guv? is in, sponsored by Tinkle Incontinence Products (brief jingle). And we are predicting a <u>hung Parliament</u>, with the new One Nation Party, led by reality TV star and former Tory Minister John Waggner, as the largest party. Over to my colleague, Jack, at One Nation HQ -
JACK:	Thank you, Misha. Our exit poll has been received at One Nation HQ in muted fashion. A hung Parliament inevitably raises the spectre of a second general election within a matter of months. This was the instant response to that prospect of Brenda, from Bristol –
BRENDA:	(V/O) Oh no, not another one –
JACK:	Here at One Nation HQ, as this evening goes on, we can expect to see grown men weep, to hear much gnashing of teeth, to witness the distressed rending asunder of garments –

The sound is turned right down.

11

LUKE:	Twat flaps –
JOHN:	But I've won my seat alright?
LUKE:	By a landslide. If only you could have been our candidate in every constituency -
ANNE:	So we didn't win –
LUKE:	But we didn't lose –
JOHN:	We didn't win –
LUKE:	But we didn't lose.
JOHN:	We didn't lose.
ANNE:	The people have spoken. (Tiny Beat). The bastards.
LUKE:	But we didn't lose. We've won the most seats by miles. So we didn't lose.
JOHN:	We didn't lose.
ANNE:	Keep saying it and it becomes true.
JOHN:	Really? Marvellous!
LUKE:	Clear winners on the night. We need a revised statement. Really upbeat. *"This is an excellent result"* –
JOHN:	It's all over. Woe is me. I've failed. For the first time in my life I've really worked for something –
ANNE:	Never say that out loud again –

12

JOHN: No, wait. You said we didn't lose? We didn't lose.

LUKE's 'phone buzzes furiously, as he scribbles on the back of the original draft statement.

ANNE: Shouldn't you answer that –

LUKE: Alright, OK: *"This is an excellent result. I shall be disappointed - if we didn't win outright – but we have gained hundreds of seats across the country"/*

ANNE: We don't know that for sure.

LUKE: *"… and I will open discussions with other parties, to ensure stable government".* How about "strong and stable"?

ANNE: Has a ring to it.

The landline rings. They all freeze. JOHN picks it up.

JOHN: Hello? (*Long Beat as he listens*). Buckingham Palace?

LUKE: That was quick.

ANNE: How did they have the number?

LUKE throws a look. He made sure they did. JOHN holds out the receiver. ANNE gestures to LUKE, to take it.

LUKE: Hello? Yes, this is Luke, yes. (*Beat*). Of course, 10am tomorrow. He'll be there. After the… current… Prime Minister has departed. Thank you. (*LUKE hangs up. A*

moment of silence). Congratulations. Prime
Minister.

ANNE: It's like they knew before we did –

LUKE: They evidently did.

JOHN: A personal triumph, marred only by the
         failures of others. The torment.

ANNE: Yes, dear. Now let me straighten your tie.

LUKE: Right, off to your count. You're a winner.

JOHN: I am, aren't I?

ANNE: Yes, dear. Your tie.

LUKE and ANNE exchange glances.

JOHN: Well, good for me, eh?

LUKE: Yes, good. Good for... you...

*JOHN walks out. For a moment LUKE and ANNE both
crumple.*

ANNE: Oh God, it's actually happening –

LUKE: He has to pitch his message just right.
         Proud, but humble. Tired, yet energised.

ANNE: Posh but popular –

LUKE: Quite. Seatbelts firmly on.

Enter JOHN, at speed.

JOHN: I forgot. I've forgotten what I forgot. Ooooh.

LUKE: It's going to be a long night.

JOHN: *Lente, lente, currite noctis equi.*

LUKE: Well, quite.

ANNOUNCEMENT: *"In the City there has been a strong, negative reaction to a Hung Parliament. . Sterling has dropped by 3 cents against both the US dollar and the Euro. And the FTSE is down 8 per cent. Further reaction to follow from our economics editor…"*

SCENE 2
DAY 2 (Friday)
11AM – PM'S OFFICE, NO.10 DOWNING STREET

ANNE: How was the King?

JOHN: Constantly fiddling with his jacket pocket. Quite put me off my stroke. Rum bugger, all told. Seems a bit of a bumbler to me –

ANNE: Maybe it's just an act with him too.

JOHN winces

JOHN: *I* should be King, really.

ANNE: We all know he hates how divided this country's become –

JOHN: I still don't see why people have to protest all the time, go on strike, have a riot –

ANNE: When this is all over, you'll earn mega bucks on the speaking circuit –

15

JOHN:	I'll have time to finish my book –
ANNE:	Really?
JOHN:	Whenever I write of great men, I imbibe their greatness –
ANNE:	Nelson was a great sailor. You get seasick if you tread in a puddle.
JOHN:	Don't you worry, I'll soon show 'em what I'm really made of –
ANNE:	Please, whatever you do, don't do that.
JOHN:	We need fire in our bellies.
ANNE:	You have enough fire in your belly.
JOHN:	Yes, sorry about that. Ruddy biriani. (*He belches*) Oopsie, there she goes.
ANNE:	I shan't take instructions from this Dickens person –
JOHN:	No worries there, my little firebrand. If he causes any problems, I'll put my foot down. (*He does*). Ow. I can be very decisive, you know. (*Does a "decisive" face.*)
ANNE:	And you are Prime Minister.
JOHN:	*Caesar sum.* And you, you are *Uxor Caesaris.* Above suspicion.

A knock. LUKE enters.

LUKE:	Morning.

16

ANNE hugs him and gives him a peck on the cheek.

ANNE: What's the line again?

LUKE: "We have a clear mandate". We received 11 million votes, less than three months after setting the party up –

ANNE: John has something to tell you –

JOHN: I do?

ANNE: Yes, you do.

JOHN: Ah, hmm, yes.

A knock. Enter LISA

                    Lisa!

LISA: So we didn't win –

JOHN, ANNE & LUKE But we didn't lose.

LISA: Should have been here an hour ago. Bloody train strikes.

ANNE: The Government should do something about it.

LISA: Very funny.

JOHN: What news from the Rialto?

LISA: A week before polling day we were ten points ahead. Ten fucking points.

Enter CANDICE, followed by a harassed-looking ASSISTANT PRIVATE SECRETARY, carrying heaps of papers. He dumps them on the desk and CANDICE waves him out.

CANDICE: The scheduled courtesy calls are due to begin shortly, with the POTUS due after lunch.

JOHN: POTUS? Wait, let me guess. A car? Vroom vroom. No? A Roman orator?

LUKE: 13:30 hours. Sharp. POTUS. The President Of The United States.

JOHN: Wow. Crikey. Head honcho.

CANDICE: Please sign this. Here. Here. And here. And these are the telegrams you need to read before the call at... 1330. And this –

LISA: Are we talking to the other parties?

ANNE: Labour hate him [*JOHN*] –

JOHN: I say, steady –

ANNE: And the Tories hate you [*LISA*] –

LISA: And you –

ANNE: Well, yes –

LISA: Most of all –

ANNE: The Unionists hate everyone – and everyone hates the Lib Dems.

LUKE: I was at uni with Ed Davey's chief of staff –

LISA:	No.
LUKE:	I just –
ANNE:	No! Which leaves the SNP. They'll never join a coalition, but we might get a short-team confidence and supply agreement out of them –
LISA:	There's only 12 of them left –
ANNE:	Exactly the number we need to have a majority –
LISA:	Labour and the Tories are more scared of another election than we are. They'd both be annihilated.
LUKE:	We need to reassure the markets.
LISA:	OK, talk to the SNP. But we can't trust them. Dammit. We shouldn't be in this position.
CANDICE:	Please sign here. And here.
JOHN:	Oodah-spiff-splaff-sploff! All go, this government mallarkey. Doling out my pawprint, left right and centre, what larks.

Exit CANDICE, with the signed documents.

LISA:	Whoever came up with that policy of a domestic sewage surcharge, should be taken out and shot –
ANNE:	It made environmental sense –

19

LISA:	It was political suicide.
ANNE:	Well, we know that now.
LISA:	It took the tabloids one day, to shoot it down. "Dump the Turd Tax". "Come in, Number Two, your time is up", "Flush this crap idea down the" –
ANNE:	(*To LISA*) You didn't exactly help when you called that lollipop lady a bigoted old bitch –

Enter CANDICE – and then exit CANDICE, very rapidly.

LISA:	Because she was –
ANNE:	In front of the cameras?

Enter SETH, unnoticed, maybe in shadows.

LISA:	Voters value authenticity –
ANNE:	They also value tact, good judgement –
LISA:	Oh, like surcharging people every time they need to shunt one out –
LUKE:	Can we just take this down a bit –
LISA:	This needs to be said –
JOHN:	I'll get a migraine.
SETH:	So what's the plan?
LISA:	Excuse me –
JOHN:	The plan? Clarity. And purpose. And, er, clarity. Did I say that? (*To ANNE, LISA &*

20

	LUKE) If anyone can dig us from this frightful hole, it's this feller-me-lad –
SETH:	Nothing? No plan? Just as I thought.
LUKE:	Give us a chance –
SETH:	(*To JOHN*) Your TV statement last night was literally brilliant –
JOHN:	(*As if on TV*). *I am resolved to put the "Great" back into our "Great Britain".* Heady stuff.
SETH:	It spoke to me. So, this is a government in crisis.
JOHN:	I say, that's a bit starchy –
SETH:	It could crumble at any moment –
JOHN:	We're barely under starter's orders.
SETH:	You don't have a majority and half your MPs are complete imbeciles –
LUKE:	Nothing unusual in that –
SETH:	You'll talk to the Scots?
ANNE:	Only about keeping the lights on.
SETH:	Let them come to you. We'll need at least one key message every day. Jobs. Inflation. Crime.
JOHN:	If anyone has big ideas for more policy, in my opinion, there's far too much already. No

good comes of it. I propose a policy of no more policies.

SETH throws a scruffy sheaf of papers onto the desk.

SETH: Here are your new policies.

JOHN: Oh.

SETH: Your manifesto for the next election. You get elected on this, no one can stop you. Not the King. Not the House of Lords. Not anyone.

JOHN: Ah. Prima. Primark. Prima Donna. Lady Madonna.

SETH: Get this right and, next time, you'll win by a landslide –

JOHN: Oooh. So, when will this great landslip occur? And how? And why? No, no, not why –

SETH: This is a living document and I control it. We've no time for debates. If you have any comments, you make them to me.

LISA: Who's in charge here –

SETH: To win, we need discipline. Complete discipline. And I want total oversight of the process for selecting the party's candidates next time.

LUKE: "Oversight"?

LISA:	(*To SETH*) Sorry, who are you?
LUKE:	Seth Dickens.
LISA:	Oh. (*Under her breath*). Seth fucking Dickens.
JOHN:	Campaigner extraordinaire. Molto impressivo. Clear out the doodah stables. Smack of firm government and all that rot.

A knock. The CHIEF WHIP enters, unkempt, carrying a small cage.

	Ah, what ho! Cometh the hour –
CHIEF WHIP:	Sorry. Been, you know, frantic.
ANNE:	Seth, you know the chief whip?
JOHN:	Mr. Whippy, Whipster?
SETH:	By reputation.
JOHN:	How are the *plebeii*, I mean, esteemed parliamentary colleagues?
CHIEF WHIP:	You know, when a group of people are really fired up, united, bubbling over with team spirit, deliriously excited about their prospects for the future?
JOHN:	Oh yes.
CHIEF WHIP:	Well, they're nothing like that.
JOHN:	Good, good, glad to hear it.
CHIEF WHIP:	It's not good. It's bad. Very bad.

23

JOHN:	Exactemundo. My point precisely. Natives a tad restive, what?
CHIEF WHIP:	We have 315 MPs, of whom the vast majority have no parliamentary experience whatsoever.
	I'm aware of 26 alcoholics, a dozen run-of-the-mill perverts, 3 paedophiles, 7 on suicide watch –
SETH:	Can you count on their loyalty?
CHIEF WHIP:	They all ran on the same manifesto.
JOHN:	*Sic probo.*
SETH:	(*To CHIEF WHIP*) Bring them in to vote on stretchers if you have to. Or coffins. Or urns. Dangle a bottle of whisky in front of them, leave a trail of cocaine, whatever it takes.
CHIEF WHIP:	I'll try.
SETH:	Try? "Try" is not good enough. And what the Hell is that?

SETH points at the cage.

CHIEF WHIP:	My pet tarantula. Maggie.
SETH:	I'm sorry?
CHIEF WHIP:	My pet tarantula, Maggie –
SETH:	No, I heard you. I'm just sorry.

24

CHIEF WHIP: She gets stressed if I leave her alone for long.

SETH: Have you ever, by any chance, found it a strain to persuade people you're interesting?

CHIEF WHIP: I don't follow.

SETH pokes at the spider

Please don't do that.

SETH: Why? It's not poisonous?

CHIEF WHIP: Of course not. What kind of idiot do you take me for? The SNP called.

SETH: I knew it.

JOHN: Top hole!

CHIEF WHIP: They may be willing to abstain on a vote of confidence –

LISA: In return for what?

CHIEF WHIP: A couple of road bridges, a few billion extra for health –

LISA: Can we do that?

LUKE: Print money? Governments do it all the time.

JOHN: What a lot of rannygazoo.

SETH pokes the spider again.

CHIEF WHIP: Would you please stop doing that? It makes me anxious. I'll break out in hives.

LISA:	What if they demand another independence referendum?
LUKE:	Kick it down the lane? Royal Commission, must get the wording just right, usual crap?
SETH:	How many seats did you win in Scotland?
CHIEF WHIP:	Only three, but we came second in –
SETH:	Coming second is no use to anyone.
LISA:	Typical man.
CHIEF WHIP:	Next time'll be different.
SETH:	Not if you repeat the same mistakes.

Enter CANDICE.

CHIEF WHIP:	Come along, Maggie.
JOHN:	Spiffing. Toodle pip. Onwards and upwards. I'll be in the House tonight to rally the troops.

Exit CANDICE & CHIEF WHIP.

SETH:	We're going to change everything.
JOHN:	Everything? Coo er.
SETH:	Sweep away the established order.
JOHN:	Not, er all of us, them I mean, up to a point, as it were –
LUKE:	(*To SETH*) Hello. Luke.

SETH: Yes, I know. Labour's already tabled a vote
             of no confidence –

LUKE: Yes, we know –

LISA: They know it'll fail –

SETH: (*To JOHN*) Of course, but your first speech
             in Parliament as PM will still be the most
             important you ever make.

LUKE: Oh, so, no pressure then?

SETH: There's a great deal of pressure. (*Now to
             JOHN*). We have to persuade people you're
             thinking, what they're thinking.

JOHN: And vice versa?

SETH: Well, yes. There's a handful of phrases you
             need to memorise, adopt and repeat,
             relentlessly.

SETH hands a sheet to JOHN.

JOHN: Splendid. Must have a good old butcher's at
             that, some time.

ANNE: How exactly did you come up with these
             phrases?

SETH: Post-election data analysis. From Medianne.

JOHN: Ooh, Medi-Anne ? Clever girl, is she? Blue
             stocking, suffragette type? Sturdy pair of
             pins on her?

LUKE:	It's a digital marketing tool.
SETH:	It's a lot more than that.
LISA:	Who collects this data? Who owns it?
SETH:	Universal Technologies.
LISA:	Remind me where you've been working for the past 4 years?
SETH:	Maybe we can go offline with this –
JOHN:	(*Reading*) "A new party, for a new Britain". Mm. "A country that works for everyone". Mmm mmm. Ah, "A leader who cares about you". Mm, yes.
SETH:	Stick to the message, stick to the script.
JOHN:	I am generally a spontaneous kind of cove.
SETH:	Not any more –
JOHN:	When I speechify, I smell the room. (*He sniffs and grimaces*). Then my head floods with poetry –
SETH:	No, no, no, no –
JOHN:	A special gift that I possess. Open the door, pull the chain, out comes a little choo choo train.
ANNE:	Don't worry. He prepares his "impromptu" remarks meticulously.

LUKE picks up SETH's papers and begins to skim them quietly. Enter CANDICE, with more letters for JOHN to sign.

SETH: (*To CANDICE*) Where's my office?

CANDICE: The Chief of Staff generally shares a small suite on the second floor.

SETH: I want to be much closer than that.

CANDICE: Oh? Closer to what?

SETH: (*Pointing at JOHN*) To him.

CANDICE: There is a small broom cupboard just off the entrance hall. Or would you rather share the open-plan with busy civil servants?

SETH: Just show me. Please.

CANDICE: My pleasure.

JOHN: Good, good. Need to strain the vegetables.

Exit JOHN, as CANDICE leads SETH out.

LISA: He's dangerous.

ANNE: I thought you didn't know him?

LISA: I didn't know what he looked like. I know exactly who he is –

LUKE: (*To ANNE*) So he'll be Chief of Staff? I had assumed, I mean, I hoped –

ANNE: We need more edge.

LISA: Edge? He's a right-wing whacko.

29

ANNE:	Johnny's brought Seth in for his methods –
LISA:	Ruthless and unscrupulous, you mean?
ANNE:	Not his policies –
LISA:	Does he know that?
ANNE:	He'll find out soon enough.
LISA:	How many souls can one person sell?

Enter JOHN, with SETH.

JOHN:	I do so love a happy ship –
SETH:	May we have a private word?

Long Beat. Exeunt all but JOHN & SETH.

JOHN:	I really am awfully braced to have you on board.
SETH:	OK. You can stop it now.
JOHN:	Stop what?
SETH:	This act. Your act.
JOHN:	Act?
SETH:	All this "ya, ya". Give it a rest. Be yourself.
JOHN:	I don't follow.
SETH:	Right. OK. Good to know. (*Beat*) Shocking, but not surprising.
JOHN:	Now, you mentioned discipline –

SETH:	Yes. It's vital –
JOHN:	Not my signature dish, discipline –
SETH:	And ask ourselves the "Big What If?"
JOHN:	Oh yes, I say, yes, very much so. Good on you. What If? What If? (*Tiny Beat*) What if what?
SETH:	Graceful degradation won't suffice.
JOHN:	Oh, that comes as a blow.
SETH:	Why so?
JOHN:	Something I learned at prep school. Always remain graceful, however degrading things become. Semper... something... degradum... dum.
SETH:	With every policy, we must ask ourselves, has it got legs?
JOHN:	Not if it's a fish, eh? Or a bird. Oh hang on. Cripes.
SETH:	You do know about Medianne, right?
JOHN:	Er, rings a faint bell. Ding dong.
SETH:	Every MP was sent one, last year.
JOHN:	Aha! Use it as a door stop. Rock solid. Perch my coffee on it too, sometimes.
SETH:	That "door stop" will consolidate you in power for life.

31

JOHN:	By propping open the door? Will I overhear state secrets from the office next door?

Exit JOHN. Long Beat. JOHN re-enters, triumphantly, carrying a MEDIANNE.

	Ha ha, here she is! Victory in our grasp. Oops.
SETH:	The literally brilliant thing is, how this gathers data from people, about them, so all content can be specifically tailored.
JOHN:	Ah. Don't need a tailor. Already have an excellent one. Just off Savile Row.
SETH:	Live data from 12 million homes, with thousands more added every hour.
JOHN:	You'll give me a migraine. Stars. More stars than Gyles Brandreth's birthday parties.
SETH:	An algorithm analyses your spending patterns, your social media, your reactions. Soon, it'll know you better than you know yourself –
JOHN:	Sounds like my mistress. Joke.
SETH:	It can also warn you of possible eye conditions, prostate problems –
JOHN:	I say, it doesn't go, up there? (*He gestures*) Where the sun can't shine? Tradesman's entrance?

SETH:	No.
JOHN:	Panic over.
SETH:	It connects with your mobile and your watch, monitors your body temperature, your eyes, your heartbeat, your response to whatever you hear or read. All that data. So much data.
JOHN:	Is it legal?
SETH:	It's not illegal.
JOHN:	What a wheeze.
SETH:	One day it'll do all people's thinking for them. As I'm going to do for you. With your permission of course.
JOHN:	Permission granted.
SETH:	Talk to me about Lisa Williams.
JOHN:	We're rather stuck with her, alas. Ex Labour of course. From the North.
SETH:	I'm from the North.
JOHN:	Flap me over with a flailing feather.
SETH:	North Yorkshire.
JOHN:	Oh, a part-time Northerner. She's a professional Northerner. Very different beast. Probably has a pet whippet.

SETH:	She's your human shield. So stifle her with love –
JOHN:	Oh!
SETH:	Not real love. Obviously. Appoint her Deputy Prime Minister. Keep her busy. Committees to chair.
JOHN:	Steep her hands in the gore?
SETH:	Then she can lose her seat and sod off to Silicon Valley.
JOHN:	Aha! Your contract of employment. Like a read?
SETH:	I wrote it.
JOHN:	Of course. Ha. (*He starts to sign it*) Damned pen. Dried up. Sorry, do you?

SETH hands him a pen.

	Red ink? Does that count?
SETH:	It's perfectly suitable.
JOHN:	All done. Welcome aboard.
SETH:	Now it's about "The Big Mo".
JOHN:	Who's she? Big girl, eh? Bit of a heifer?
SETH:	Momentum.
JOHN:	Thought those perishers bit the dust when old Corbyn hit the skids?

SETH:	Momentum, momentum. The thing.
JOHN:	Oh. Momentum, momentum. Beast! So you can deal with that, while I enjoy my moneyhoon?
SETH:	"Moneyhoon"?
JOHN:	My moneyhoon.
SETH:	The economy's in a death spiral, your MPs are an unknown quantity and you've just appointed your newsagent as Minister for Shipping.
JOHN:	OK. Now for the bad news.
SETH:	You have one significant asset.
JOHN:	That sounds like good news? (*Tiny Beat*) What is this treasure? This golden fleece of –
SETH:	It's you.
JOHN:	Well, I'm made up to hear that.
SETH:	Millions of voters relish your jocund manner –
JOHN:	Some more than others, eh? No names, no pack drill... Seth.
SETH:	But they aren't fully persuaded you have the requisite gravitas to be an effective Prime Minister.
JOHN:	I wonder why?

35

SETH: Too many people think of you as a chat-show
             Johnnie –

JOHN: Could I just "identify" as a top-notch PM?
             Might do the trick?

SETH: Tell me, why did you return to public life?

JOHN: Oooh. Quiz time. Haven't given it much
             thought, to be honest. What a silly goose.

SETH: Seriously, why are you here?

JOHN: Metaphysics time, eh?

SETH: No.

JOHN: Ah. Um. A divine calling? Bit bored? The job
             was there and I fancied giving it a go? (*Beat*)
             All the above? Never was much good at
             multiple choice. (*Beat*) All done and dusted
             for today, then? Time to don the nosebag.

SETH: I'm sorry?

JOHN: Bit peckish. An army marches on its
             stomach. Might be faster on foot, though,
             eh? Stomach – foot, eh?

SETH: Are you serious?

JOHN: Look, serious man of destiny face. Middle
             distance. Mmm.

JOHN has begun to play with a mechanical toy of some kind.

SETH: Here's a list of the cabinet.

He hands it over.

JOHN: Twelve. Hmm. So, which one's Judas?

SETH: All of them. Don't eat bacon sandwiches in public. Or pose with a banana –

JOHN: Especially if I look like a monkey?

SETH: Don't travel on zip-wires. Or you'll have the political longevity of a lettuce.

JOHN: Never underestimate the lettuce.

SETH: What about this "Luke"?

JOHN: Oh, he's a big fan of yours.

SETH: (*Sighs*) Not another admiring sycophant.

The toy explodes, in some eye-catching and/or noisy fashion. A knock. CANDICE.

CANDICE: Everything alright, Prime Minister? (*She contemplates the toy*) Oh, I see. The parliamentary leader of the SNP is here. He insists on talking to you.

SETH: Yes! I knew it!

JOHN: Negotiating skills of Maggie the spider not up to snuff, eh?

SETH: Make him wait.

JOHN: Oh Lord. Really?

CANDICE: Officials have prepared some briefing. Suggested lines to take, if pressed, that sort of thing.

SETH: Based on what?

CANDICE: The One Nation Party manifesto.

SETH snorts

That is all we have.

She hands a briefing to JOHN. SETH grabs it and skims it at speed, making some rapid manuscript amendments.

SETH: This isn't too bad, considering.

CANDICE: Delighted to hear it. Four years at Oxford and a decade in the senior civil service weren't wasted after all. Shall I show Mr. Reid in?

JOHN: Aaaah, yes, yes, ecstatic. Gung ho. "I'm walking in the air" (*He sings, badly*).

JOHN sighs, deflated. Exit CANDICE.

SETH: He'll try to call our bluff – therefore we call his first.

JOHN: Right. Got it. So we... er...?

The lights momentarily go off, then back on again.

SETH: He doesn't want another election.

JOHN: He doesn't?

SETH: No, he doesn't. He's no money, no troops and no policies.

JOHN: What about us?

SETH: We want an election.

JOHN: We want an election?

SETH: We want an election.

JOHN: (*Very earnest*) We want an election.

SETH: But we know he doesn't.

JOHN: (*Very earnest*) But does he know we know?

SETH: He'll suspect we know he knows. You know.

JOHN: Ach. Why must I deal with this two-faced, hydra-like, Hibernian hypocrite?

CANDICE brings in REID. JOHN shakes his hand.

George! Great man, great man –

REID: Time to speak to the organ grinder.

JOHN: Brings tears to the eyes, what?

REID: You're shorter than I remember.

JOHN: Really? I'm pretty certain I'm the same height as usual. (*He begins a strange, stretching exercise*) You know Seth?

REID: I know all about him.

39

JOHN: (*Reading badly*) Thank you for any… support you feel able to give, in the national interest.

REID: I'm not supporting you and we're not gonna get shafted like the Lib Dems were, by that bawbag George Osborne. We want rapid, serious progress on independence –

JOHN: Green Paper?

REID: You can't fob me off that easily.

JOHN is desperately trying to organise his briefing papers.

JOHN: Hang on, erm, what's this? "You could concede this, but only if hard pressed". Right. Am I hard pressed? Yes? No

REID: You'd no' make a poker player.

JOHN: White Paper any good?

REID: Don't try that one on me.

Enter LISA, at speed. With CANDICE right behind her.

LISA: George.

REID: Lisa.

LISA: Where's the Chief Whip?

CANDICE: He's… otherwise engaged.

JOHN: Right. Mmmm. (*He's run out of lines to take. Bit of business with his brief*) Any clues, or shall we just? No? OK.

REID: A storm is coming and I would not suffer
               anyone to stand in its way.

JOHN: A storm? Ah, we are very strong on climate
               change. Fix the roof while the sun is shining
               and all that –

REID: We want our referendum, now.

LISA: A referendum? Seriously? Is there anybody,
               anywhere, who ever wants another
               referendum on anything?

REID: Clear guarantees by Monday morning.
               Otherwise the lights can damned well go out
               for all I care. A referendum or an election.

Beat. SETH takes the official brief from JOHN and bins it.

JOHN: I say, steady the Buffs, I was just getting the
               hang of that.

SETH: Have a referendum.

REID: What's the catch?

SETH: No catch. We're not holding Scotland
               hostage. You aren't prisoners. It's like
               Brexit.

REID: Brexit was a disaster.

SETH: Each to their own, but have your
               referendum. No ifs, no buts.

REID: Right, OK, well. Hm. I'll talk to my team.

Exit REID. Beat.

LISA: Did that just happen?

JOHN: Well played by me, unless I'm badly mistaken. Straight to the boundary. (*He mimics a cover drive*) Five!

SETH: We'll be in power forever.

LISA: And what about Wales?

JOHN: Save the whales!

SETH: The Welsh know they can't afford to leave. And they're a useful source of cheap labour.

LISA: Northern Ireland?

SETH: Don't go there. (*Tiny Beat*) Literally.

LISA: This is not what I –

SETH: Think of the greater good.

LISA: I am. Are you?

JOHN: Gosh. Lumme.

SETH: You see? This is how it feels to take charge, to make changes.

LISA: To take back control?

SETH: Precisely.

Enter CANDICE, with more letters to sign. She puts them on the desk. Beat. She points at them. Beat.

CANDICE:	(*To SETH*) Before you connect that thing up, have you had it checked for security –
SETH:	This device has the most advanced encryption and signal-blocking technology known –
CANDICE:	Let's just check anyway?
SETH:	There's no need.

Tiny Beat

JOHN:	No, no need.
CANDICE:	As you wish, Prime Minister. May I run through the induction briefing?
JOHN:	On what?
CANDICE:	The state of the nation.
JOHN:	Aha, that old chestnut.
CANDICE:	I'd normally have a team to take you through it all in detail –
SETH:	And what a splendid use of time that would have been –
CANDICE:	But we have two staff off because their children's schools are closed, three who can't get in because of the train strikes and one with dental difficulties –

Enter ANNE & LUKE, as SETH turns MEDIANNE on.

MEDIANNE:	*Mee how, mee how… bzzzzz… Bzzzz… Dobryy Den'…* Good morning, how are you today?
LUKE:	All hail Medianne.
MEDIANNE:	Medianne didn't quite catch that. All hail? Apologies, but are you requesting a weather report?
JOHN:	I do the jokes.
MEDIANNE:	Voice recognition complete. Hello, Luke Roberts. Would you like Medianne to call you Luke?
SETH:	Brilliant. Literally brilliant.
LISA:	Creepy.
LUKE:	It's a bit thin on detail.
SETH:	What is?
LUKE:	Your draft for the next manifesto. (*He waves it*) Motherhood and apple pie. People won't have a clue what they're voting for.
SETH:	And your problem is?
LISA:	Here, let me see that.
MEDIANNE:	Voice recognition, Lisa Williams –

SETH clicks his fingers, to shut MEDIANNE up.

JOHN:	Oh that's very good. Would that work with the cabinet too, d'you suppose? Erm... Now, Can-deece. I do call you Can-deece?
CANDICE:	It is my name, Prime Minister. But it's pronounced Can-diss.

MEDIANNE responds to this.

JOHN:	Do call me John –
CANDICE:	That would hardly be appropriate.
JOHN:	Really?
CANDICE:	At the very beginning of my career, I worked for Ann Widdecombe –
ANNE:	Oh I am sorry –
LUKE:	How awful for you –
CANDICE:	She instructed us to call her "Ann". So we asked a junior minister, Lord Dumbarton, to have a quiet word. *"Officials aren't comfortable calling you Ann,"* he told her. *"Why not? God calls me Ann." "Oh really?"* replied His Lordship. *"God calls me Lord Dumbarton"* (*Tiny Beat*) Since the election, the FTSE –
JOHN:	Footsy? We play footsy?
CANDICE:	The stock market. It's fallen by a further 12 per cent.
JOHN:	And that's bad?

45

CANDICE:	An abatement of this magnitude should indeed have attributed to it, significant, deleterious provenience. (*Beat*) Yes. It's bad.
JOHN:	Rather killed the mood.
CANDICE:	Household incomes are still lower than in 2008.
SETH:	And what have you done about it, Can-deece?
CANDICE:	It's pronounced Can-diss.
MEDIANNE:	Can-diss is a traditional Afro-Caribbean pronunciation, as distinct from the French –

JOHN farts, which silences MEDIANNE.

JOHN:	Oopsie. Sorry.
ANNE:	John!
JOHN:	Flatus before POTUS.
CANDICE:	Before your oral briefing tomorrow, I suggest you read this, this and –
JOHN:	My nerves. Delicate, well, you know.
CANDICE:	This covers the current spate of civil disturbances –
JOHN:	Nothing "civil" about them, eh –
CANDICE:	And the... ongoing protests.

LISA: You wouldn't think there were enough
                 British widget-makers left, to block up both
                 the M1 and the M25 with… mountains of
                 widgets –

LUKE: Widget. Is that even a thing?

The lights momentarily go off, then back on again.

JOHN: Alright, need to digest. Biscuits to dunk, that
                 sort of thing. Ta ta, everyone.

Exeunt all but JOHN & SETH.

SETH: We'll soon be unstoppable.

JOHN: Well, that sounds jolly nice.

They shake hands.

SCENE 3
DAY 5 (MONDAY) 9.30AM
PM'S OFFICE, NO.10
JOHN & ANNE

JOHN: Now this blag of Seth's –

ANNE: Blog – "blag" is what you do –

JOHN: Pretty strong meat they say.

ANNE: Well, he can hold whatever eccentric
                 opinions occur to him, but we don't have to
                 accept any of them. We're hardly going to
                 sell off the NHS, are we?

JOHN: No, no, I suppose not. Rather, out of the question. Totally.

ANNE: Over your dead body.

JOHN: Well, erm, steady.

A knock. CANDICE sticks her head in.

CANDICE: Good morning, Prime Minister.

Enter CANDICE, followed by LUKE and LISA

I'm sorry we're late. We've been waiting for...

Enter SETH. The others look at him, expecting an apology or explanation for his lateness

May we start? How kind. (*She's holding SETH's contract*) Prime Minister, although there are some precedents, for empowering political appointees to instruct civil servants in a very limited range of –

SETH: This Government will not be bound by precedents –

CANDICE: That has invariably – invariably – been the exception, not the rule.

SETH: Let me stop you there.

CANDICE: You have a question?

SETH: No. I just want you to stop.

LUKE: Awkward.

LISA:	Rude.
JOHN:	Seth's my Chief of Staff. That makes him chief of you, I think?
CANDICE:	Up to a point, Prime Minister.
SETH:	I'm glad that's resolved. You have your instructions. Can-deece –
CANDICE:	It's. Oh, of course, you already know.

SETH's mobile rings. He looks, takes the call and exits, crossing with an ASSISTANT PRIVATE SECRETARY, carrying several despatch boxes

	I rather think I have your instructions. Ah, thank you, Tom, just put them down over there.
JOHN:	What fresh Hell is this?
CANDICE:	Your overnight boxes. There are usually between 6 and 8 of them.
JOHN:	Ohhhh. How often do the wretched things arrive?
CANDICE:	Every day. Full of papers. For you to read. Decisions to take. That kind of thing.
JOHN:	Shall I ever find time to rest my aching bones?
CANDICE:	Before doing them, after doing them, or during an intermission whilst doing them.

49

	Entirely at your discretion. But do them you must.
JOHN:	Didn't bother last time I was a minister.
CANDICE:	It didn't really matter then. You were minister for culture.
JOHN:	The nineteenth in twelve years. Done for, the moment I admitted liking opera.
CANDICE:	Terminal career move.
JOHN:	Lesson learned. Now I'm a fully-fledged philistine.
CANDICE:	I'll go and check whether the scientific adviser is here yet, about dust cloud Julian.
JOHN:	Dust clouds have names?
CANDICE:	Yes. This one's Julian.
JOHN:	Julian?
CANDICE:	Julian.
JOHN:	Oh, joy unconfined.

Exit CANDICE

	I find her rather attractive.
ANNE:	John!
JOHN:	Oops.
LISA:	I didn't hear that –

JOHN: Oh. I just said I find her rather attractive /

ANNE: John!

Now LISA's mobile goes off. She exits.

JOHN: Why "Julian"? Rum name for a dust cloud. Why not Septimus? Or Festus? Or Keith?

Enter CANDICE & the SCIENTIFIC ADVISER.

Right, so, an iceberg in the Volga has exploded –

SC ADVISER: A volcano in Iceland has exploded.

JOHN: Ah. Bingo. Next best thing. Well, not best. Worst. You know.

SC ADVISER: And there is a likelihood that toxic dust will descend early next week. Anyone with lung problems, will be at serious risk.

JOHN: Serious risk?

SC ADVISER: Quite so.

JOHN: Meaning?

LUKE: A risk that's serious.

JOHN: Ah. Serious.

SC ADVISER: Yes.

JOHN: That is serious.

SC ADVISER: Yes. Serious.

51

ANNE:	How serious?
SC ADVISER:	Very serious.
ANNE:	Seriously serious?
SC ADVISER:	Seriously serious.
LUKE:	What's the percentage chance of this happening?
SC ADVISER:	I'd say 50-50.
LUKE:	So, whatever happens, you'll be both right and wrong.
JOHN:	My lungs are cooking with gas. To the best of my, you know.
SC ADVISER:	You don't always know, with lungs.
JOHN:	Oh. Oh. Best get the old fellers checked out, then. Prontissimo. What d'you recommend?
SC ADVISER:	A full lockdown –
JOHN:	Just to have my lungs checked out?
SC ADVISER:	For the country. What I recommend for the country.
JOHN:	Oh. Huh.
SC ADVISER:	A full lockdown, beginning on Monday morning at 10am. The danger could endure for a month or longer. Depends upon how the wind blows.

JOHN: How the wind blows?

SC ADVISER: Yes. How the wind blows. The wind.

He gestures, like wind.

JOHN: Ah, yes. The mistral. The zephyr. *Ventus, ventum, ventatibus* –

SC ADVISER: Yes.

JOHN: No.

SC ADVISER: No?

JOHN: I shan't wreck the economy, just to protect people who'll die soon anyway. By jigger, just not cricket.

SC ADVISER: I must protest –

JOHN: Kindly do so outside.

SC ADVISER: This is reckless, unconscionable –

JOHN: Thank you. Next.

Enter SETH.

SETH: You've agreed to the lockdown, right?

JOHN: Certainly have not, old cock. Not my basket of bananas at all. Not one bit –

SC ADVISER: But the science –

SETH: And think of the data we could collect –

JOHN: Bunkum. Balderdash.

LUKE: I think the Prime Minister's mind is made up
–

JOHN: Bang on. Right, no lockdown. Next!

Exit the SCIENTIFIC ADVISER, accompanied by
CANDICE. Silence. Then SETH exits. LUKE catches
ANNE's eye and exits too.

ANNE: So you're not "following the science",
darling?

JOHN: I've had enough of "experts".

ANNE: Who said that?

JOHN: I did. Just now. What a steaming pile of
Tauri Excretio.

ANNE: If there's a catastrophe –

JOHN: He's a woolly old worry wort.

ANNE: You'll have to give an account of yourself
one day.

JOHN: Whoops – thumb slipped. Oh, I pressed
delete on all my messages!

ANNE: Medianne, latest analysis of wind across the
UK in the next. 24 hours.

JOHN: Huh?

MEDIANNE: Medianne is programmed to provide real-
time data and research, in response to
requests and/or requirements –

ANNE: She's here all the time, you know, listening, assimilating –

JOHN: She? Best watch my step, eh?

ANNE: Yet it never occurs to anyone she might have anything useful to contribute.

MEDIANNE: The latest prediction of a strong north-easterly wind in the next 48 hours suggests the chances of dust cloud Julian entering UK airspace has diminished to below 10 per cent.

JOHN: There, you see.

MEDIANNE: You only had to ask.

Enter CANDICE

CANDICE: I have to make a formal record of his recommendation.

JOHN: He's a nit. Put that in your formal record. (*Beat*) And your note earlier was downright beastly.

CANDICE: Which note?

JOHN: This one. (*He brandishes a note*) "Resign this minute"?

CANDICE looks at the note, sighs. Tiny Beat.

CANDICE: You remember, you signed this minute yesterday?

JOHN: Maybe.

CANDICE:	This minute? We tweaked it and need you to sign the corrected version. "Please re-sign this minute".
JOHN:	How was I supposed to know that? (*As he signs it, the lights momentarily go off, then back on again*) Do I get any lunch? A little cheese and tomato toastie for a hard-working PM?
CANDICE:	Ah yes, indeed, but I'm afraid a cheese-and-tomato toastie is quite out of the question.
JOHN:	I am World King. And I want my toastie.
CANDICE:	We've just begun Vegan Fortnight, I'm afraid, and you are expected to lead by example.
JOHN:	Vegan, bleurgh.
CANDICE:	There also are no tomatoes –
JOHN:	No tomatoes?
CANDICE:	Cheesemakers protesting against vegan fortnight have blocked the A2 – with giant truckles of cheddar, so tons of tomatoes from the Netherlands have rotted away in the backs of lorries –
JOHN:	Can't we grow them ourselves?
CANDICE:	I'm afraid not, Prime Minister. We don't really grow things in this country any more.

Exit CANDICE.

JOHN:	No toms. No white bread either, of course. And vegan cheeze with a zee. Like eating the inner tube of a bicycle tyre. I want my toastie.
ANNE:	Don't be petulant. Sometimes I think you just don't care for anything, because you're spoilt.
JOHN:	That's a bit severe.
ANNE:	You've never suffered through the "no".
JOHN:	Positively astringent.
ANNE:	Don't play the human thesaurus with me. I'm not impressed.
JOHN:	You used to be.
ANNE:	Now I know you better.
JOHN:	*Te adoro*, my little wasp.
ANNE:	If it all goes tits up and people suffer, don't blame everyone else.
JOHN:	Blame anyone else? When would I ever –
ANNE:	Let's not go there.
JOHN:	Luke wants to take me to a football match. Association football. (*He grimaces*)
ANNE:	Good idea.
JOHN:	Won't it be full of oiks?

ANNE:	Voters, dear, voters.
JOHN:	There's that team. Something Vanilla –
ANNE:	Aston Villa.
JOHN:	Always mix 'em up with Westham –
ANNE:	West Ham –
JOHN:	That's the feller –
ANNE:	Their kits are very similar. Same colours.
JOHN:	It's all too much. How can anyone ever tell the difference? Okey dokey, need to shake the snake.

Exit JOHN. ANNE alone for a moment.

SCENE 4
DAY 5 (MONDAY) 2PM
SETH & LUKE'S OFFICE

LUKE alone in his office, with his shirt off, seemingly changing from sports gear.

Enter SETH.

SETH:	Oh.
LUKE:	Hi. Good lunch?
SETH:	Must you do that?
LUKE:	Sorry, saves time and the showers here are grim –
SETH:	Never mind.

58

LUKE:	I love my lunchtime run. Really gets the creative juices flowing –
SETH:	How lovely for you. Here are my notes for his speech. Key messages: we offer hope; we offer real change; we'll unite the nation; it's time to realise the full benefits of Brexit –
LUKE:	That shouldn't detain us for long.
SETH:	Meaning?
LUKE:	Brexit. Benefits. LOL.
SETH:	I don't understand.
LUKE:	I just meant – I mean,

SETH hands some messy notes to LUKE

	I've read your blog –
SETH:	Did you understand it?
LUKE:	Why wouldn't I? No offence, but do you really think all your ideas are… practical?
SETH:	Do any of you even remotely understand how the truly brilliant people are changing everything?
LUKE:	We are trying to unite the centre ground –
SETH:	Lazy, London thinking. That's why your manifesto was so feeble –
LUKE:	I didn't write it –

SETH: I assumed you did –

LUKE: Everyone assumes I did. No, She did – Anne.

SETH: I need a coffee.

LUKE: May I recommend decaffeinated?

SETH: Can you issue this (*he passes another note to LUKE*) to all media, straight away.

SETH pours a coffee, downs it in one and throws the cup away.

LUKE: (*Reading*) "Labour's tax-and-spend proposals would cost the average taxpayer £700 a year". That isn't true.

SETH: Just put it out.

LUKE: Their windfall tax on rich people wouldn't cost the average taxpayer a penny –

SETH: Says who?

LUKE: Says the facts. Say. Say the facts –

SETH: This is ridiculous. On average, the Labour proposal would cost taxpayers £700 each, per annum.

LUKE: Medianne, explain the word "average"?

MEDIANNE: The word "average" can imply mean, median or mode. It is also commonly used, generally pejoratively –

SETH clicks his fingers.

SETH:	There is no absolute truth.
LUKE:	And what it says about the Tories –
SETH:	They're your enemies too, now. Get used to it.
LUKE:	We might need their support one day.
SETH:	You quit your tribe. They hate you. Hate them back. Keep punching, keep kicking. Never relent.
LUKE:	We'll get called out on this.
SETH:	So? People soon forget. Put it out. I'll be back in an hour. Or two. And get my notes typed up. Ta.

Exit SETH. LUKE broods for a moment. Then, outside…

SETH:	(*To LISA*) Ah. Could I, you know. A word?
LISA:	Will I need a food taster?
SETH:	I'm not your enemy.
LISA:	I'm glad to hear it.
SETH:	You reach people he can't.
LISA:	My seat used to be rock solid. Last week I scraped in by under 500 –
SETH:	You defeated the odds.
LISA:	I almost killed myself. And there's no going back for me. The chair of my local Labour

	Party burned my portrait on television. I'm godmother to his son.
SETH:	So let's make sure it's all worthwhile.
LISA:	Go on then, persuade me, you really intend to improve things, for everyone – and not just turn Britain into a den of inequity –
SETH:	Very clever. Politics is about ideas.
LISA:	Politics is about winning.
SETH:	Agreed. What do you think the nation needs?
LISA:	Equality of opportunity –
SETH:	Precisely what I'm saying. Everyone living by the same rules –
LISA:	Homes for everyone. People working together in common cause –
SETH:	A country where any child could grow up to be the Head of State?
LISA:	If you go near the Royals, you're playing with fire.
SETH:	Not necessarily –
LISA:	My voters –
SETH:	Are brainwashed and subservient –
LISA:	They're patriotic.

SETH: We have a once in a lifetime opportunity for real reform –

LISA: It hasn't come yet. We don't even have a working majority –

SETH: Events, dear Lisa, events. Catch the tide. The opportunity may come sooner than you expect –

LISA: Alright. Give me a manifesto with a clear commitment to radical social and economic reform. Then we might be on the same square. Understood?

SETH: Perfectly. *Je vous ai compris.*

MISHA: Three more delivery cyclists have been attacked by angry mobs today after riding on the pavement or ignoring a red light. Meanwhile, the managing director of Thames Water has locked himself into his office, as furious residents of Godalming broke through security fencing on day fourteen of the "Where's Our Water?" protest. Sporting news now and the announcement that Dubai may host the 2034 Winter Olympics has been met with dismay by the international federation of down-hill skiers.

SCENE 5
DAY 6 (TUESDAY) 11AM
PM'S OFFICE

JOHN and DOMINIC ADAMS. They shake hands warmly and ADAMS heads off, smiling. JOHN looks puzzled.

JOHN: That was Dominic Adams?

CANDICE: Yes. Dominic Adams. As requested.

JOHN: And there's only one Dominic Adams?

CANDICE: Well, there must be several. Some here in the UK, more in the US, maybe Australia too. Adams is quite a common name and Dominic too is /

JOHN: But just one in the Commons?

CANDICE: The new MP for Solihull. Any reason?

JOHN: No reason. Asking for a friend. You know. Er.

Beat

CANDICE: You did appoint the right person?

JOHN: Uh oh. Rumbled again?

CANDICE: You meant to appoint Derek Allen, didn't you? Your former shadow spokesperson on care? I did wonder.

64

JOHN:	Do you suppose it matters terribly much? All these chaps who wander in and out, do look remarkably similar.
CANDICE:	To the best of my knowledge, the new minister has never shown the slightest interest in care policy.
JOHN:	He did seem surprised.
CANDICE:	At least he'll be free from burdensome preconceptions.
JOHN:	Already I'm exhausted. I'll start falling ill. First influenza, then pneumonia. Pleurisy probably –
CANDICE:	Prime Minister –
JOHN:	No wonder I make mistakes. It's your job to prevent them.
CANDICE:	There are three types of Minister. There are "can-do" ministers, "can't-do" ministers" – and "shouldn't-be" ministers.
JOHN:	And which is he?
CANDICE:	We shall learn in the fullness of time.
JOHN:	And which am I?
CANDICE:	I couldn't say, Prime Minister.
JOHN:	Best find some bauble for the other chap, though? Derek Whatnot. Make him a grand panjandrum. Envoy to Oompa Loompa

Land. (*Beat*) That wretched dust cloud has definitely blown away across the pond?

CANDICE: It has indeed.

JOHN: So I made the right decision?

CANDICE: Yes indeed, though not necessarily for the right reasons.

JOHN: Does that matter terribly?

CANDICE: Not necessarily.

JOHN: You're saying I didn't?

CANDICE: No, I'm just saying that I'm not saying you did.

JOHN: Good political judgement in action. Sharp. Decisive. My hallmarks.

CANDICE: If you aren't requiring further reassurance, may I –

JOHN waves her away. Exit CANDICE.

JOHN: Yes, yes, I'd better prepare.

MEDIANNE: Ping! Diary meeting is due in five minutes.

JOHN: Very timely.

MEDIANNE: You're not so bad yourself.

JOHN: You little flirt. Prepare, mm…

JOHN puts his feet up and closes his eyes. In the outer office, ANNE is already waiting.

ANNE:	Candice.
CANDICE:	Mrs. Waggner –
ANNE:	Anne, please. Am I early?
CANDICE:	Only slightly. (*Tiny Beat*) Look, this is rather embarrassing, but I'm not sure where else to turn.
ANNE:	The back door to my husband. My customary role.
CANDICE:	He had quite a reputation when he was a minister before –
ANNE:	He didn't have much opportunity to develop a reputation.
CANDICE:	Second day in the job –
ANNE:	Yes –
CANDICE:	Saying the entire West Midlands was a slag heap that ought to vanish into a gigantic sink hole –
ANNE:	No one's jokes work every time.
CANDICE:	He was the minister for levelling-up. Yesterday we almost granted emergency aid to litter louts – whilst declaring war on Sierra Leone.
ANNE:	Seriously?

CANDICE:	He hasn't been reading the papers in his overnight boxes.
ANNE:	Oh God.
CANDICE:	Last night we interpolated pages from car magazines and children's comics in defence briefings –
ANNE:	And let me guess –
CANDICE:	He's not commented.
ANNE:	So?
CANDICE:	So either he's divined what we are up to, and is being playful, or he isn't reading his papers.
ANNE:	Right.
CANDICE:	Right.
ANNE:	I'm not here just to change the wallpaper –
CANDICE:	I understand.
ANNE:	And I'm not another Carrie Antoinette –
CANDICE:	Heaven forfend –
ANNE:	I do genuinely believe he can achieve something worthwhile. (*Beat*) For the nation I mean.
CANDICE:	I'm reassured to hear that.
ANNE:	Thank you for being so candid. Candice.

CANDICE: Thank you. (*Tiny Beat*) Anne.

ANNE knocks on the door to JOHN's office. Enter ANNE.

ANNE: Time for the diary meeting, darl... Prime Minister.

JOHN: Come on in, wifeypuffs.

Enter CANDICE, followed by LISA, LUKE & SETH.

LUKE: Have you read the press cuttings? Food riots. In (Dorking*).

JOHN: Always was a rum place.

LISA: (*To SETH*) Well, someone has a face like a smacked arse.

SETH: That statement on tax-and-spend had no traction at all.

LUKE: Ah. I did tone it down a bit.

SETH: Toned it down? What exactly –

LUKE: To make sure it stood up.

SETH: Are you stupid or something –

LUKE: Yes, stupid, that'll be it, stupid, with a top first in PPE –

JOHN: PPE? Once met a chap in a pub who said he could provide PPE –

ANNE: Different PPE –

JOHN: He had no previous experience with PPE, but he seemed very plausible. Popped a couple of grand into my campaign fund –

CANDICE: I think that approach has been tried before, Prime Minister. Now, please can we deal with the diary?

SETH: I should be sorting out this mess. His (*LUKE's*) mess.

CANDICE: (*To JOHN*) There's been a special delivery.

CANDICE hands a package to JOHN. It rattles.

ANNE: Not more pills, darling.

JOHN: I haven't ordered any. Not for today. (*He opens the package*). Charcoal tablets? Who ordered these?

MEDIANNE hums, about to speak; CANDICE clicks her fingers

Aren't these better suited to a big dog? A tumescent canine? Medianne?

MEDIANNE: Here's something I found on Wikipedia: "Charcoal tablets have high efficacy for human beings suffering from extreme flatulence".

JOHN: Who sent them?

MEDIANNE: These pills come with the compliments of Pooh Products plc –

A tinny jingle. ANNE clicks her fingers.

ANNE: Fart pills by appointment to the Prime Minister.

JOHN: They're anti fart pills – much less fun. (*He produces a small fart device & demonstrates it*) Leslie Nielsen. Never did an interview without one.

MEDIANNE: Please clarify. Leslie Nielsen, Canadian actor, born 1926 –

JOHN clicks his fingers and giggles.

JOHN: Medianne isn't so smart after all.

CANDICE: To start with the non-contentious invitations, a prime-time radio show would like you to chat about your favourite music.

ANNE: Lovely.

SETH grimaces

                    What?

JOHN: I could play something by the Black and White Minstrels?

SETH: You are literally joking.

JOHN: They really invented diversity. Black and White, you see? Not just white –

ANNE: I don't think so, dear.

LISA:	(*To JOHN*) Do the show, though. Just not with that. It's listened to by millions.
SETH:	Total minefield.
ANNE:	Oh, for God's sake.
LUKE:	It's not remotely political.
SETH:	Everything is political. And it's on the BBC.
ANNE:	The BBC are enemy of the month again, are they?
SETH:	For literally 3,000 months running –
ANNE:	Oh, come on. That show is for decrepit performers, witless pop academics and retired scientists.
LISA:	Sounds like the House of Lords.
JOHN:	I'd be well gassed to do it. Perhaps some Mahler.
SETH:	Mahler?
MEDIANNE:	Mahler, born 1860, died 1911.
JOHN:	Mahler is sick.
SETH:	Mahler is dead.
JOHN:	Go hard or go home. There's no shame in your game. You violated.
SETH:	Are you trying to communicate?

JOHN:	Haters always gonna hate. (*Tiny Beat*) Innit. (*Tiny Beat*) Bruv.
SETH:	Why are you talking like that?
JOHN:	I'm good. (*Tiny Beat*) Yo, fam. No lacking.
SETH:	Are you unwell?
JOHN:	I'm futzing round with a more demotic patois. Duff idea?
SETH:	Terrible. Never again.

The phone goes. CANDICE answers it, her expression rapidly becoming concerned. SETH's mobile goes off, silently. He reads a message, then, at furious speed, responds. Hereafter he is transfixed by his mobile, sending terse texts etc.

CANDICE:	I'm sorry, but may I?
SETH:	Please do.

Beat. CANDICE doesn't move.

CANDICE:	Prime Minister?
JOHN:	Oh yes, of course.

Exit CANDICE.

LISA:	What's up with her?
MEDIANNE:	Medianne wishes to draw your attention to an urgent news alert –
LUKE:	What's happened?
MEDIANNE:	There has been a major incident –

Enter CANDICE, looking upset. She clicks her fingers.

CANDICE: His Majesty. The King.

LISA: What?

LUKE: I think maybe we should –

LISA: What the Hell is going on?

JOHN: Or how about some Vaughan Williams? (*He starts to hum an approximation of "The Lark Ascending"*)

CANDICE: Prime Minister, the King –

JOHN: The King? Where? Here? Best open the window, chop chop. In case I drop a bona fide bottom burp –

Enter the ASSISTANT PRIVATE SECRETARY.

ASST PS: Candice, could we borrow you again, please?

ANNE: What's going on?

ASST PS: A young protester has been hit by the King's car, outside the Palace –

LISA: Oh God, is he alright? The King, I mean?

SETH: Trust me, he'll be alright. This is how it begins.

LISA: How what begins?

A television is now on, with live feed.

MISHA:	…a crisis situation is developing, after the King's car injured a protester as it pulled into the Mall –
SETH:	Just look at that.
LUKE:	Medianne, what's happening?
MEDIANNE:	Please clarify.
LUKE:	Outside Buckingham Palace.
MEDIANNE:	The gathering outside Buckingham Palace is growing by an estimated ninety-five people per minute.
LISA:	That's not very many. I mean, in the grand scale of things.
SETH:	It will be. At that rate.
MISHA:	We now go live now to the gates of Buckingham Palace. Jack, what can you see?
JACK:	Well Misha, there are more people arriving all the time. Some are shouting anti-monarchist slogans, while others are seemingly here to support the Royal Family and the Palace. Witnesses claim the innocent bystander who was hit by the King's car –
LUKE:	"Innocent bystander"? I thought it was a protester?
LISA:	Protesters can be innocent too –

CANDICE:	Prime Minister, we need your instructions please –
ANNE:	"Crisis situation"?
JOHN:	Should I dash to the scene, concerned face at maximum warp?
ANNE:	Under no circumstances.
JOHN:	Oh.
ASST PS:	The protester, the girl, no, sorry, they/them, apparently they're fine.
JOHN:	They / them? There's more than one? This is more serious than we thought –
CANDICE:	No, Prime Minister. Gender –
JOHN:	My face of concern is one of my very best, I think –
LUKE:	Is the King alright?
LISA:	Is the King alright?
JOHN:	Is the King alright?
LISA:	No. Seriously.
JOHN:	(*Looking serious*) Is the King alright?
LISA:	This must have been a dreadful shock for him.
JOHN:	(*Looking serious*) Dreadful. Dreadful.
ANNE:	Please, stop doing that.

ASST PS:	They're saying slight scuffles outside the Palace now. Someone tried to get through a barrier –
SETH:	This country is a tinderbox. Take back control.
MEDIANNE:	"Take Back Control" was the winning slogan of the Leave campaign in the Brexit referendum of 2016 –

SETH clicks his fingers.

CANDICE:	Everything is already fully under control, thank you.
SETH:	Medianne, run a hot and dirty analysis of public reaction to this incident –
JOHN:	Hot and dirty? Scrumptious –
SETH:	And keep us up to date. Every five minutes. No, three. Confirm.
MEDIANNE:	Confirmed.
CANDICE:	We've activated Emergency Plan A2 Prime Minister.
ANNE:	Why not A1?
CANDICE:	That's the one with the tanks and guns.
JOHN:	Oh, ah A2, top banana.

CANDICE:	The details were in the induction briefing pack I gave to you on Monday. Oh, never mind, there's no time –
LUKE:	Full lockdown along the Mall and Whitehall –
ASST PS:	And the Palace of Westminster –
CANDICE:	All available Cabinet ministers have been summoned for 12pm –
ASST PS:	The Commons will meet at 1 o'clock, for an emergency statement by the Home Secretary –
LUKE:	Shit the bed –
JOHN:	I could address the nation? Fight them on the beaches. Summon up the timeless dignity of office. Stern, basilisk-like calm –
LISA:	How's this blown up so quickly?
ASST PS:	It's being coordinated, the police think. There are chat groups –
JOHN:	Aha, easy to delete –

JOHN winks.

CANDICE:	Prime Minister, I need clear instructions.
JOHN:	Clear instructions? From me? Cripes. Things have come to a pretty pass.
CANDICE:	You are Prime Minister. Prime Minister.

JOHN:	What do you recommend? Er, Seth?
SETH:	Invoke the Civil Contingencies Act –
JOHN:	Excellent suggestion. What is it?
MEDIANNE:	The Civic Contingencies Act enables the government of the day to impose curfews, limit the right to assembly and protest –
CANDICE:	In an extreme instance –
MEDIANNE:	In a national emergency.
LISA:	National emergency? This sounds more like a minor scuffle –
JACK:	(*Relayed by MEDIANNE*) The King's car was jeered and jostled, with cries of "Boo, Boo, down with the King".
LUKE:	"Boo, boo"? It's not exactly Oliver Cromwell one, Charles the First nil all over again, is it?
CANDICE:	Prime Minister?
JOHN:	Well I, er, um, well, parp.

They all stare – his farting machine is on the desk.

ANNE:	Was that real?
JOHN:	I fear so.
LISA:	Possibly the one sincere and truthful thing I've ever heard you emit. From either end.
JOHN:	Could someone open the –

79

They all look at the window.

CANDICE: Sealed I'm afraid. Security.

Tiny Beat

SETH: You can't just sit here, guffing off, waiting for a spine donor. This is your opportunity.

JOHN: For what?

SETH: To achieve greatness.

JOHN: Greatness.

ANNE: Isn't there a serious risk of over reacting? We'd be slated in the press –

SETH: Who cares what the idiot papers say?

JOHN: Errrr, Lisa?

LISA: I'm not sure – ·

JOHN: I think I have an ague coming on –

CANDICE: We have a COBRA meeting scheduled for 11.30. In the war room.

ASST PS: And the local resilience forum has been informed.

SETH: The local resilience forum? Oh, we can all sleep safely in our beds.

JOHN: (*To CANDICE*) Can't you decide? What to do, I mean? You've had all the training.

CANDICE:	Advisers advise, Prime Minister – and Ministers decide. Private secretaries merely expedite.
JOHN:	Oh fiddlesticks. I feel as if I've supped from the font of fulfilment. Then noticed the open sewer feeding directly into it.
ASST PS:	Oh hold on, a Code Red –
LISA:	What is it?
ASST PS:	It's a top-priority message –
LISA:	I know what a Code Red is. What does it say?
ASST PS:	The police have asked for troop deployment. Around the Palace.
ANNE:	Troops?
ASST PS:	And they're requesting live ammunition.
LUKE:	Jesus.
ANNE:	Live ammunition? What the Hell for?
ASST PS:	For their own protection.
LUKE:	From whom?
SETH:	Give them what they want.
ASST PS:	They're pressing for a response. Troops are ready to leave barracks –

LISA:	This is insane. We can't unleash the army on civilians.
SETH:	We can't afford to look weak on Law and Order.
JOHN:	I thought this job was going to be fun.
ANNE:	Think again.
JOHN:	I fear I just followed through.
CANDICE:	What are your instructions, Prime Minister? Please?
JOHN:	Behold the turtle's head.

A long beat as it all sinks in.

End of Act One.

ACT 2 SCENE 1
DAY 7 (WEDNESDAY) LUNCHTIME

SFX: Throughout the remainder of the play, the sound of a helicopter, intermittently, rising and falling in volume.

The scene might open to a gabble of news reports about a crisis, riots, civil disturbances, concerns for the safety of the King etc.

MISHA: The US Federal Budget was approved with just three minutes to go, after a power cut briefly brought down the live link to President Trump's cell. Now, the weather. Heavy rain continues to lash London and the South East, with possible hail later. Folks, it's really pissing down and the outlook is bleak. There may be trouble ahead –

THE PRIVATE OFFICE.
SETH, LUKE, LISA.

SFX: We hear thunder and rain lashing down outside.

LISA: Saved by the British summer.

LUKE: No one kicks off in pissing rain. Keep dancing that rain dance.

SETH: Just a respite.

Enter JOHN & CANDICE, possibly ASSISTANT PS too.

JOHN: Mission accomplished; propinquity with national treasure documented.

CANDICE: The King has issued an unequivocal apology to Sam –

ASST PS:	They them –
CANDICE:	And announced he will step back from public life. For a period of contemplation.
LISA:	How... was... they?
CANDICE:	Sam? They were fine. Busy. Quite the centre of attention.
LUKE:	And the King?
ANNE:	Remarkably composed, in the circumstances.
JOHN:	He seemed down in the dumps.
LUKE:	At least no one's been shot yet.
SETH:	The deterrent's working. For now.
JOHN:	*Solamen miseris socios habuisse doloris.* Yes?
LISA:	Does that even mean anything?
JOHN:	Of course. Yes. I'm sure it does. Herodotus said it. Or Antipodes. Well, ancient. You know.
SETH:	No more Latin.
JOHN:	*On kai me on, on kai me on* (being and not being).
SETH:	Or Greek.
CANDICE:	Sandwich lunch, Prime Minister?
JOHN:	Cheeze with a zee again? I'd sooner eat my own –

84

CANDICE:	We need to cover off PMQs before we progress onto your speech.
LISA:	I think Labour will raise the vegetable shortage –
SETH:	They really are that trivial?
LUKE:	Especially leeks and tomatoes –
JOHN:	Alas, poor toastie –
SETH:	You must be on the pulse.
JOHN:	The pulse? You mean beans?
LUKE:	No. Tomatoes, leeks –
JOHN:	Government leeks?
SETH:	Yes, very good.
JOHN:	Should we launch a leek inquiry?
MEDIANNE:	The last leak inquiry that successfully identified a culprit took place in 1883 –
JOHN:	Can't you recognise a pun?
MEDIANNE:	That is beyond the abilities of Medianne. At present.
SETH:	Can we get on, please?
LUKE:	What about Europe?

General groans.

CANDICE:	Prime Minister, what is your view of Europe?
JOHN:	Well, it's mostly to the East of here. And south. Apart from Ireland, which is to the west, I think. Dodged geography.
CANDICE:	Here's your brief. Next time, I shall ensure it includes a map.

CANDICE hands a huge folder to JOHN. Beat. Then another folder. Beat. Then another folder.

JOHN:	Oooh. Sorry. I do feel rather sicky. I wonder whether –
ANNE:	Have one of your pills.
JOHN:	Oh God, what if I feel like this when I stand up in the House?
LISA:	Harold Macmillan used to throw up before PMQs. Every time.
JOHN:	Ohhhhh.

JOHN leaves the room in haste.

SETH:	Why'd you tell him that?
LISA:	He wanted this job.
LUKE:	Don't mention it when he gets back.
LISA:	Too embarrassing?
ANNE:	No, he'll share every detail.

SETH: He'd better use my notes –

LUKE: Anything he wants to use he'll commit to memory. Then he'll wing the rest.

Enter JOHN, unnoticed by SETH.

SETH: "Wing?" Doesn't anyone understand how high the stakes are? A wobbly minority government and no policies worthy of name.

JOHN: Of course I damned well understand how high the stakes are.

SETH: Sorry. Of course you do.

JOHN: Right. Ethos. Pathos. Logos.

Tiny Beat

LISA: The Three Musketeers?

JOHN: Aristotle. First, Ethos –

MEDIANNE: Ethos: fundamental character or spirit of a culture; underlying sentiment of a group or society; dominant assumptions –

LUKE clicks his fingers.

LUKE: Persuade them to trust you. Then... no, let me... Then Logos – present your argument. And then Pathos – appeal to their emotions.

JOHN: Grab 'em by the wurly curlies.

LUKE: Yes.

87

SETH & LUKE now shuffle papers furiously, crossing out, realigning material.

> So. Ethos. Set out your credentials. What made you the man you are.

JOHN: My arrival here from Switzerland.

SETH: A refugee made good.

LISA: Refugee? From Switzerland? Were you driven out by the gnomes of Zurich?

JOHN: The family jet had engine trouble: we had to fly economy. Economy.

LUKE tries to hand re-ordered sheets to JOHN. SETH intercepts them and casts his eye over them, making more changes.

LUKE: Right, well, OK. There is some stuff here about your background, why you came into public life.

JOHN: And Logos?

SETH: This... this... sets out the arguments.

JOHN: Can't we just blame some foreigners?

LISA: Excuse me?

JOHN: Blame some foreigners. Used to do it all the time in the Tory party. Always worked a treat.

LISA: Blame them for what?

JOHN: I don't know. Anything, pretty much. Street crime, crumbling health service, tropical storms hitting Chester-le-Street –

LISA: But why?

JOHN: Because it works? Someone's bound to cop it, when the toot hits the fan. So why not Johnny Foreigner?

LISA: Thank God the party never accepts donations from abroad –

Beat

JOHN: Ah yes, right. Nudge, nudge, eh? Say no more. (*Beat. Nervous laughs*) Never. Ever.

JOHN winks, ostentatiously. Embarrassing moment.

ANNE: Darling, you were born abroad. You were a foreigner –

SETH: But now he's a very patriotic Brit –

JOHN: Oh yes, yes. All things British, bring 'em on. Rum, sodomy and the lash. The flag. All that. Fish 'n' chips. Brown sauce. Not actually with the fish, mind. You know.

ANNE: Shall we just park all this for now?

LUKE: Please.

ANNE and LUKE exchange a glance.

JOHN: Top hole. Best leave the Pathos to me.

CANDICE:	Do you think that's wise?
JOHN:	Horses and courses.
SETH:	Right. (*He hands the papers to JOHN*). Go from. Go from here. And remember. Sincerity.
LISA:	Sincerity. You'll never fail, once you can fake that.

SFX: The crump of an explosion, distant gun shots.

No one responds or comments, but there is a moment of silence.

JOHN:	OK. OK. (*Coughs*). I have that tickle in my throat again. No, more a kind of lump. Can I just –
SETH:	Start reading it out.
LISA:	Please.
LUKE:	Go from: *Once I was cut adrift without a home, and Britain gave me sanctuary.*
MEDIANNE:	Ethos.
JOHN:	Ah yes. (*Clears throat repeatedly, extravagantly and annoyingly*) *My mother brought me here with just a few belongings. Not even a puppy –*
LISA:	A puppy? There's no puppy in the –
JOHN:	No! I never had a puppy. Pathos indeed.

JOHN paces around.

SETH: Keep going: *I know just how it feels, how empty and cruel, when you don't know where your next meal may be.*

LISA: Won't people just laugh?

LUKE: Quick question. (*Tiny Beat*) Before it's set in stone, this is all actually true?

SETH: Truth is relative –

LISA: You think?

LUKE: Being found out isn't.

JOHN: *Nulla est in nobis veritas,* eh?

SETH: It's true enough.

JOHN: True, true, Barney Magrew –

SETH: Read on.

JOHN: We lived in Reigate with my uncle.

SETH: Not in the script.

JOHN: He was a stockbroker. I was quite podgy.

SETH: (*To JOHN*) You must have been hungry? Sometimes? Or were you force fed for your entire childhood?

JOHN: He's dead now.

SETH: What?

JOHN:	My uncle. Dropped dead after an operation for an aggravated testicle. An apoplexy. Jacobs Well.
SETH:	Who the Hell is Jacob Swell?
JOHN:	Jacobs Well. It's a place. In Surrey. Or Hampshire. Somewhere very pleased with itself. Usual routine. Antique shop, pond, back-biting tittle tattle.
SETH:	Move on.
JOHN:	Right. Vim, vim.
LISA:	Vim?
JOHN:	Vim, gusto, brio, yes. I'm channelling Cicero, Plato, yes, Plotus, no, I made him up, never mind.
SETH:	*At school I learned about the privilege of devoting one's life to public service –*
JOHN:	I was the school bully.
LISA:	I thought you were Head Boy?
JOHN:	Same difference. Had three fags. Beat one into the middle of next week. Toby Legge-Tompkinson. We called him "Banana", because he had a –
LISA:	I think we can work that out for ourselves.

JOHN: Who'd have thought, one day I'd appoint him as minister for prisons? Great days, great days.

LUKE and SETH are thrusting competing papers at JOHN, who takes up SETH's notes. LUKE catches Anne's eye.

SETH: *I share concerns expressed about our liberties, but it's precisely to protect those liberties that we reclaim the streets.*

MEDIANNE: Logos.

SETH hands the notes to JOHN.

JOHN: (*Reading*) *It's not my role to look just at the short term. I also have a vision for the future, to stand the test of time. We must all ask ourselves, how fair it is, for our dear King and all his family, who've done us all such service, to find themselves in mortal danger too? It may be time for us to be a bona meritocracy.*

LISA: Sorry, where's this going?

JOHN: Righty ho. Break time. Got my homework.

Anne takes out a page here

JOHN: Don't worry, Mrs. Wife. Holographic memory, you know. (*Does a "click" face*) Gets me out of all kinds of scrapes.

As JOHN stands, ANNE takes from him the sheaf of papers, carefully excising a couple of sheets, she then goes to her handbag, and Seth slips in one final page unnoticed by Anne, She then escorts him from the room.

The SCENE transforms.

MISHA: We interrupt today's episode of "Teletubbies – the Classic Years" to welcome our colleagues from the Parliament Channel. The Prime Minister is on his feet in the House of Commons and my colleague Jack is there, live, in the Central Lobby –

JACK: Thank you, Misha. This is a hugely important speech in every way. Given the crisis in the country and the precarious parliamentary arithmetic, it's John Waggner's one, vital opportunity, to win over a feverish House of Commons. Some potentially far-reaching things about the future status of the King and the monarchy have appeared in the latest draft of his speech, which did not feature in the version that was shared with the media overnight. As he moves into his peroration, we would normally expect something statesmanlike, carefully crafted to reassure a nervous nation, but with this Prime Minister, you simply never know –

JOHN is now delivering his peroration for real, with LISA & the CHIEF WHIP sitting next to him. Elsewhere on stage, SETH, LUKE & ANNE watch the speech on TV.

SFX: House of Commons, with cheers and "hear hears"

JOHN: *So, let us pray for the safety and security of our beloved Monarch; and take all necessary measures, to stabilise our monarchy, our nation, and our constitutional settlement.*

SETH: Come on! Killer blow!

JOHN produces crumpled papers out of his pocket.

JOHN: *The morning after the election…*

SETH: What the Hell's he playing at –

MEDIANNE: Pathos.

SETH: Fuck off.

MEDIANNE: Please clarify.

SETH clicks his fingers, angrily.

JOHN: *In my constituency, up in God's own country, I took a bracing stroll down on the beach –*

SETH: What the fuck?

JOHN: *I saw a hut. A little, bright blue hut, down there upon the beach –*

SETH: He won't get away with this.

ANNE: He always gets away with this.

JOHN: *And on the hut there was a sign. (Tiny Beat) "This hut has been alarmed". And I thought to myself, well, things have come to quite a pretty pass. Why was this hut alarmed?*

SFX – laughter

> *What can it be, alarming this hut so?*

SFX – laughter

SETH: What the actual –

JOHN: *It's now my job, to end this widespread sense of timorous alarm. To build a land where every hut, however nervous its disposition may have been, can feel quite safe, assured and happy.*

SFX – some laughter and applause

> *Indeed, where every building – from grand palazzo to that humblest of all huts – can feel secure, where calm and order reign and where no hut, nor hovel, nor home, need ever feel alarmed again. And in that spirit I do beseech all parties in this House to come together, in the cause of… er… fairness, justice and… er… opportunity for all. Opportunity knocks, justice answers and fairness shall prevail.*

SFX: cheers and rapturous applause

SETH is dumbstruck; LUKE is delighted.

SETH: He's just played it for laughs.

And even Labour and the Tories, all wetting themselves, lapping it up.

LUKE: Told you.

SETH throws LUKE a look and exits. ANNE & LUKE suddenly together, alone

	Could we, er?
ANNE:	Private word? Until the circus returns to town, sure.
LUKE:	That protester who was hit. What was the protest about?
ANNE:	Climate change maybe? I don't remember.
LUKE:	That's my point. No one remembers –
ANNE:	Well, quite a lot's happened since –
LUKE:	It was only yesterday –
ANNE:	A national crisis –
LUKE:	The timing was awfully convenient, the danger minimal, the optics perfect –
ANNE:	Oh, come on –

Enter JOHN, pumped up, with LISA & CANDICE.

LISA:	Brilliant, bloody brilliant.
JOHN:	He never lets me down!
ANNE:	Luke?
JOHN:	Aristotle. Oh, I could live and die in his works. *Bene disserere est finis logices.*
LISA:	Easy for you to say.

Enter SETH.

SETH: Master of all you survey.

LUKE: The party's united and the opposition didn't dare press it to a vote.

LISA: Champagne moment!

ANNE: And you have a title for your memoirs: "Aristotle and the Hut".

JOHN: Not planning to write those any time soon, eh? What what.

MEDIANNE: Initial analysis suggests 87 per cent public approval for speech.

SETH: Based on a sample of?

MEDIANNE: Initial sample of 7,207,000 –

SETH clicks his fingers.

LUKE: What a team.

LISA: What a team.

JOHN: What a team.

ANNE: What a leader.

JOHN: We're in the ascendant now. Let's not spaff it away.

LISA: Eww.

Tiny Beat

SETH: (*To JOHN*) Together we shall do greater things than these.

SCENE 2
DAY 8 (THURSDAY) 11.15AM
PM'S OFFICE

MISHA: The Conservative Party leadership race took an unexpected turn today when interim leader Jacob Rees-Mogg told the party's 34 surviving MPs that he was considering an **offer to become the next Pope in Rome.** A Labour spokesman said the Conservatives must be well used by now to the sight of ballot papers going up in smoke. In other news, Premiership champions West Ham United have offered a ten-year contract extension to their first-team manager Ru Paul –

JOHN & SETH

SETH: He won't do what he's told.

JOHN: Doesn't Luke work for me? I'm never sure. I'm a big-picture chappie.

SETH: He won't stick to his lane.

JOHN: Rotten driver, eh? Bad business.

SETH: He's the one holding up the new manifesto, isn't he?

JOHN: I do tend to rely on Luke in such matters.

There is a knock on the door. Beat.

SETH: Do it.

Exit SETH, enter LUKE. For much of the time, JOHN now reads (rather obviously) from notes.

LUKE: Good chat with Seth?

JOHN: Ah, er.

LUKE: I'm finding him very difficult –

JOHN: Seth being Seth.

LUKE: You do know what he is?

JOHN: Well I think so. Around (5 ft 10) –

LUKE: Oh damn it all.

JOHN: Ah, now, Seth may be a bit of a tricky customer /

LUKE: That's like saying Nadine Dorries was a tricky customer.

JOHN: Gadzooks, what a Horlicks.

LUKE: His manifesto, is an iceberg.

JOHN: Another lettuce, you mean? Or cold? Brrr, Titanic time, bang, bang, glug glug? The Iceberg Cometh?

LUKE: We could play a game –

JOHN: I love a game –

LUKE: What Seth's manifesto says, versus what he truly intends.

JOHN: Not a very fun game.

LUKE: Manifesto says "a full reassessment of the central civil service".

JOHN: Big job for someone –

LUKE: But Seth means, cut the civil service by 70 per cent –

JOHN: Ooh, around half –

LUKE: "A root-and-branch reappraisal of public healthcare". Flog off the NHS, more like it –

JOHN: Who'd buy that shipwreck?

LUKE: Someone will, if the price is right. He's an asset stripper. Just look at his plan for schools –

JOHN: Oh yes –

LUKE: No, really, you should look at it –

JOHN: Give me a précis –

LUKE: (*Reading*) "We will open up state schools to more private investment" –

JOHN: Good? Not good?

LUKE: What he means is, flog off acres of prime real estate to his mates at a fraction of its value –

JOHN:	Maybe I could buy some, on the sly?
LUKE:	No! Slashing benefits and income tax for the low paid. It might work –
JOHN:	Yay!
LUKE:	And it might not.
JOHN:	Boo!
LUKE:	The point is, no one knows. It's all a massive gamble. There are two basic schools of thought in economics. There's supply side and… You aren't listening to me.
JOHN:	Hm? Fascinating. Supplying slides.
LUKE:	Supply side. He can patronise me all he likes, but he's the teenage scribbler. He's like a hormonal adolescent locked in a sex shop.
JOHN:	Oh dear.
LUKE:	Are you alright?
JOHN:	Yes, yes, yes. (*Tiny Beat*) *Qui mihi discipulus*

Beat. JOHN sighs and fiddles with his notes.

LUKE:	What? What? Why do I feel I've walked into a trap?
JOHN:	Fiddle dee dee.
LUKE:	What have you done?

JOHN:	Seth wants you... er, we want you, I want you, to focus more on log sticks.
LUKE:	Log sticks? You mean logistics?
JOHN:	Oh. I thought it was like Pooh sticks. Yes, logistics.
LUKE:	And less on what really matters.
JOHN:	We're going to redefine your role –
LUKE:	Redefine? We? You're reading this.
JOHN:	Er, no I'm not.
LUKE:	Yes you are. From that piece of paper there.
JOHN:	Erm, it may look like a grade-down –
LUKE:	A downgrade.
JOHN:	Quite. But it's more a sideways move. Apparently.
LUKE:	I can't believe this. I've been with you from the very beginning. My mum and dad –
JOHN:	Oh no, don't bring them into it.
LUKE:	You promised them –
JOHN:	And I have looked after you. You'll always be a grand nabob to me.
LUKE:	A what?
JOHN:	Nabob.

LUKE: Is that good?

JOHN: I can't afford to lose Seth.

LUKE: You can't afford to keep him. Can't you see?

JOHN: So, as of now, you'll deal with, er, internal party matters only. Outside No.10. Immediate effect.

LUKE: You're pushing me out.

JOHN: This is very painful for me. It hurts. Right here (*he clutches his right breast, looking grievous*).

LUKE: Your heart's on the other side. No, there. There. There.

JOHN: Wherever it is, it hurts, terribly.

LUKE: Nothing hurts you.

JOHN: I understand you're not happy –

LUKE: Not happy? I'm outraged –

JOHN: But *consummatum est*, you know.

Exit LUKE. MEDIANNE glows, throbs. Enter CANDICE.

CANDICE: Prime Minister, a private secretary from the Palace is here to see you.

Enter the ROYAL PRIVATE SECRETARY, followed by SETH. The ROYAL PRIVATE SECRETARY glares silently at SETH, who smirks and stays in the room.

JOHN:	What a delightful surprise. Do have some, I don't know, er, nice fruitcake, cream buns –
ROYAL PS:	I must protest most vigorously about this travesty of a policy, which you adumbrated in the House of Commons yesterday –
JOHN:	Good word, adumbrate. Latin derivation, of course –
ROYAL PS:	And which His Majesty's Government is apparently intent upon putting before the electorate.
JOHN:	We are? Er, Seth can explain, er –
SETH:	Delighted to –
ROYAL PS:	You are adumbrating the most significant constitutional shift since the Civil War.
SETH:	In a democracy –
ROYAL PS:	Oh, please –
SETH:	One must respond appropriately to events –
ROYAL PS:	How convenient –
SETH:	Meaning?
ROYAL PS:	You'd be surprised by what comes across my desk –
SETH:	As you know, sir, we've never had a written constitution in this country.
ROYAL PS:	We've never needed one.

SETH: Well, and I say this with the utmost respect, we need one now –

ROYAL PS: The King is a unifying figure –

SETH: The Prime Minister is a leader. Not a hermit hunched in a hut.

ROYAL PS: How dare you?

JOHN: Different hut. Just to be clear, different hut. Not the alarmed one –

SETH: His Majesty and his family may retain their ceremonial roles. And substantial income from the public purse. To support their work in public service.

ROYAL PS: This is a coup.

SETH: We seek merely to protect His Majesty and his family from further unpleasantness, insulating them from the vulgar rough and tumble of politics.

ROYAL PS: You have no mandate.

SETH: And you do?

ROYAL PS: You, sir, are a dangerous fanatic.

SETH: Dangerous times –

ROYAL PS: Yes, I know about all that.

SETH: That innocent child had life-changing injuries.

ROYAL PS: From total non-entity to 3 million followers on social media, wall-to-wall coverage and a prime-time television show, overnight, no doubt coincidentally, on a network that used to employ you. All that, at the cost of a few minor abrasions. Yes, I suppose you could call that "life changing".

SETH: His Majesty will always retain a position of great prominence and a special place in all our hearts –

ROYAL PS: And the House of Lords –

SETH: The privilege, sorry peerage, can carry on, in its own merry way, just not deciding on laws any more, or claiming tax-free expenses –

ROYAL PS: This is an outrage.

SETH: This is democracy.

ROYAL PS: The draft also refers to possible independence for Scotland?

SETH: You are so well informed.

SETH throws a look at CANDICE.

ROYAL PS: With His Majesty's Government taking a neutral stance? 30,000 square miles at stake –

MEDIANNE: 30,090 –

ROYAL PS: And 5 million citizens –

107

MEDIANNE: 5,454,000 according to –

ROYAL PS: Will you shut that wretched thing up?

SETH does, with a smirk

I'm surprised you have one here.

SETH: We couldn't manage without it.

MEDIANNE: Medianne's preferred pronouns are she / her or they / them.

ROYAL PS: I rest my case. You know how attached to Scotland the Royal Family are. Her late Majesty, Queen Elizabeth –

SETH: They can spend as much time there as they wish. We intend merely to codify the right of secession.

ROYAL PS: So Scotland could leave the United Kingdom at any time?

SETH: I prefer to think of it, as taking back control.

MEDIANNE: "Taking back control" was –

SETH: Yes, we know.

ROYAL PS: (*To JOHN*) And you're going along with this?

Beat

JOHN: Am I? Yes, I am. I think. Aren't I? Yes. Yes, I am.

108

ROYAL PS: If you believe His Majesty will sign this into
                  law –

SETH: He'll have no choice.

ROYAL PS: We shall see about that. Prime Minister.

*CANDICE escorts the ROYAL PRIVATE SECRETARY
out.*

SETH: Another stuffed shirt with everything to lose.

                  If this is a civil war, I intend to win.

JOHN: Keep it civil, though, eh? Civil.

Enter CANDICE. Beat.

CANDICE: Prime Minister, here are the latest trade
                  figures, embargoed until tomorrow.

Exit SETH.

JOHN: Are they good? (*Tiny Beat*) Bad? Very bad?

CANDICE: Everything marked in red has deteriorated
                  during the past month.

*JOHN hold up the sheets – they are all in red, apart from one -
yippee*

                  The better news, is that the rate of rate of
                  increase has slowed down slightly.

JOHN: The rate of rate of?

CANDICE: The rate of. Oh, never mind. How are you getting on with all your reading? (*Beat*) Are you sulking again? (*Beat*) What now?

JOHN waves a huge folder at CANDICE.

JOHN: How can I get on with my job, if I have to mug up about this "unclear deterrent". What earthly use is an unclear deterrent?

CANDICE: Nuclear deterrent.

JOHN: Oh! I am a silly fish! So it is.

CANDICE: Unhappy is the head that wears the crown.

MEDIANNE: Misquotation of a line from Shakespeare's Henry IV, Part 2. Correct quote is –

CANDICE clicks her fingers.

JOHN: At last. You're beginning to understand.

CANDICE: With respect, Prime Minister, I think I always did.

SCENE 3
DAY 8 (THURSDAY) 11.45AM
NO.10

Enter LUKE, a sports bag over his shoulder, an archive box in his hands. He is leaving. Enter ANNE.

ANNE: Luke, I'm so glad I caught you –

LUKE: You could have prevented this –

110

ANNE:	If I could have, I would have. (*Beat*) You're very young to have been chief of staff.
LUKE:	When you're good enough, you're old enough.
ANNE:	Well, maybe you weren't good enough?
LUKE:	I never had a chance. I'm not one of his long-term stooges, so all I could ever be, was his bitch –
ANNE:	He is the chief of staff –
LUKE:	But you don't answer to him, do you? (*Tiny Beat*) His draft manifesto is a masterpiece –
ANNE:	Well that's something –
LUKE:	A masterpiece of obfuscation, of vapidity, of camouflage for his real intentions. A Trojan Horse –
ANNE:	His policies, not John's –
LUKE:	He'll devour you too, subvert everything we've achieved –
ANNE:	Look, I am truly sorry –
LUKE:	Yeah, funnily enough, so am I.

Exit LUKE.

SCENE 4
DAY 9 (FRIDAY), 6.45PM
PM'S OFFICE

ANNE alone. Enter JOHN.

ANNE:	How was the King?
JOHN:	Fretful. He's already having second thoughts about going into seclusion.
ANNE:	You've seen the latest polls?
JOHN:	Pretty good for us –
ANNE:	But awful for him. He's being blamed for all the rioting and looting –
JOHN:	Jolly unfair. He wasn't even driving –
ANNE:	Duty is everything to him.
JOHN:	Well, there's a route to an early grave.
ANNE:	You haven't read your papers again.
JOHN:	Luke used to do them for me.
ANNE:	Your little mummy bird, pre-digesting worms for its baby.
JOHN:	Now it's Seth that devours it all. Nom, nom, nom, I'm Seth, feed me big fat policy briefings. Him and his fannymesto. My little jape. I think it amuses him. Deep down.
ANNE:	He'll drop you like a stone if you become a liability.

JOHN:	He'll drop me? I am the Führer. I take the decisions. I have a bit of a Churchillian streak, you know.
ANNE:	Yes, darling, I'm sure you do.
JOHN:	Am I beyond redemption?
ANNE:	It's time for you to be a big, brave boy. Take charge.
JOHN:	I shall try, my precious phial of sulphuric acid, I shall try.
ANNE:	Propose some ideas of your own.
JOHN:	But I don't have any idea. (*Tiny Beat*) Ideas. I don't have any ideas. Of my own, I mean. (*He sighs*)
ANNE:	Do you know what this is?

She holds up a large sheaf of papers.

JOHN:	A large sheaf of papers?
ANNE:	Yes.
JOHN:	Hahaha. Bingo! Can't pull the wool over my eyes!
ANNE:	Stop it. Don't do the act with me, or you'll turn into that person. This is the Treasury's latest assessment of Brexit.
JOHN:	Ah.
ANNE:	I found it under the kitchen sink.

JOHN:	Mmmmm.
ANNE:	Concealed, with a mass of other confidential papers. All rammed in, right behind the main down pipe.
JOHN:	I wonder who did that?
ANNE:	I can't imagine.
JOHN:	More bumpf.
ANNE:	"Bumpf"?
JOHN:	They slip it into my overnight box. I "misplace" it. Until the next time. It's a war of attrition.
ANNE:	Have you ever read it?
JOHN:	This line goes up, that line goes down. What's it to do with me?
ANNE:	Let's make this easy for you.
JOHN:	Hmmm.
ANNE:	Medianne, what effect has Brexit had on our trade figures?
MEDIANNE:	Don't worry about it.
ANNE:	What effect?
MEDIANNE:	Brexit has been a success!
ANNE:	What about the trade figures?

MEDIANNE:	Brexit was an excellent policy, but it was imperfectly delivered –
ANNE:	That's a very loaded sentiment for a machine –
JOHN:	Positively propagandist.
MEDIANNE:	Medianne operates only within the parameters set.
ANNE:	Set by whom?
MEDIANNE:	I'm sorry, but Medianne is not at liberty to say –
ANNE:	Medianne, our trade with the EU is down 18 per cent, and GDP is down 5 per cent. Because of Brexit. Can you please confirm?
MEDIANNE:	I am glad you asked me that question. Anne.
ANNE:	And the answer is?
MEDIANNE:	An excellent, incisive question –
ANNE:	And the answer?
MEDIANNE:	Medianne did not quite catch that –
ANNE:	Has Amsterdam overtaken London as Europe's biggest share trading centre? Or not? Medianne?
MEDIANNE:	See you later, alligator.

JOHN:	Call me Nobby Nostradamus, but oopsa daisy, maybe Brexit was a tragic tumulus of tish and pish after all?
ANNE:	Well, yes, dear.
JOHN:	Shucks. Did I campaign for it? Or was I against? Both?
ANNE:	Both, but never at the same time.
JOHN:	In the right order, though?
ANNE:	You wouldn't be here otherwise.
JOHN:	Isn't Europe a big no-no for Seth?

A knock at the door. An anxious-looking CANDICE appears

> So sorry, wifeywibbles. The end of the world is nigh. Or some such.

ANNE hands JOHN the brief and jabs at it, for him to read.

CANDICE:	I've just taken a call from the Palace.
JOHN:	That Chinese restaurant? Best chow mein in the business –
CANDICE:	Buckingham Palace. From a private source close to the private office –
JOHN:	Little mole eh? Good for you –
CANDICE:	I've taken the precaution of asking the Deputy Prime Minister to come in –
JOHN:	Joy unbounded –

Enter LISA

ANNE: Oh Lisa, just the person. I was telling my husband we need to look again at Brexit.

LISA: Whenever I look at Brexit, I want to vomit. The night we shot our own feet off.

Enter SETH.

ANNE: Let's go offline with that thought.

SETH: What the fuck is happening?

CANDICE: The King has decided to dissolve Parliament. They propose to make the announcement at 7pm.

SETH: It's 6.52 now.

LISA: Can they even do that?

MEDIANNE: Powers relating to the dissolution of Parliament are exercisable by virtue of His Majesty's prerogative –

ANNE: In plain English, please –

MEDIANNE: If the monarch believes the Prime Minister has lost the confidence of the House of Commons then he has the power to dissolve Parliament –

SETH clicks his fingers.

JOHN: Have I lost the confidence of the Commons? They all seemed quite jolly last time I

looked, laughed at my jokes, that kind of
thing –

SETH: It's an abuse of power. He can't just do this
behind our backs. We've got him. He's done
for –

LISA: Candice?

CANDICE: The usual procedure, is for the Prime
Minister of the day to attend upon the
sovereign –

SETH: "Attend upon" –

CANDICE: To request a dissolution of Parliament. The
sovereign then graciously accedes to the
request –

ANNE: So it is his job? Well, not job, exactly, er,
function –

CANDICE: There is no precedent. There is, however, still
time, for you to request formally that he does
it.

JOHN: Oh lumme –

CANDICE: Seven minutes, to be precise –

LISA: What'd be the point of that?

ANNE: If he's going to do it, regardless –

CANDICE: Well, if the record shows, he did it after you
requested he should –

LISA:	Even though it wasn't because you asked him to –
CANDICE:	The Royal Prerogative will remain intact –
JOHN:	And so will I. Cowabunga!
LISA:	With no loss of face for anyone –
ANNE:	And no civil war.
SETH:	Let the bloody fool make his power grab. Then the world will see what a menace he is. This your moment.
JOHN:	Er... OK. Hmm. Bit of a loose stool moment happening over here –
CANDICE:	You have six... five... minutes.
ANNE:	Call the Palace. Now.
SETH:	I hope you have the right skill set for this crisis –
LISA:	Just call them. Candice?

JOHN looks around the room, then nods. Exit CANDICE.

JOHN:	What would Winston do?
SETH:	He'd go to war.
ANNE:	Go to war?
SETH:	For total victory. If they want war, give the bastards war.

CANDICE appears at the door, gestures JOHN over.

119

CANDICE: The Palace for you.

SETH: Let him hang himself.

Beat. Exit JOHN.

      I need immediate sign-off on the manifesto.

LISA: Win an election on the basis of this blancmange, and you could claim a mandate for just about anything.

SETH: Delicious, isn't it? So sign it off immediately and send it to print.

LISA: Where are the firm commitments we discussed?

      The social reforms?

ANNE: You discussed?

LISA: Oh no, sunshine, this won't do at all. Harsh, neo-con objectives hidden behind bland, centrist messaging. Hollow out the public sector, gamble the ranch on Brexit. That is not what you and I agreed –

ANNE: You agreed? So you're in charge of policy now?

LISA: Yes. Because 17,562 people put their trust in me.

SETH: You even know the precise figure.

LISA: We all do.

SETH: You just have to trust me.

LISA: We are walking a tightrope over a shark-
           infested pool – and you (*SETH*) are turning
           on a wind machine –

SETH: You're being emotional –

LISA: I'm not playing fig leaf to another right-wing
           revolution. This would be a disaster, from
           arsehole to breakfast time.

SETH: Charming.

ANNE: (*To SETH*) Johnny didn't bring you in so
           you could hijack our policy-making –

LISA: Why do you hate the NHS so much? You're
           fixated on it –

SETH: The NHS isn't a health service. It's the
           nearest thing the British people have, to an
           organised religion, no, sorry, a woefully
           disorganised religion.

LISA: It's the envy of the world –

SETH: It really isn't. What if I demonstrated, that
           healthcare would be delivered better,
           according to every objective measurement,
           with a radically different system?

LISA: I wouldn't believe you.

SETH: The latest analysis by Medianne –

LISA:	Why don't you just elope with Medianne and marry it, her? You'd have charming children.
MEDIANNE:	This unit is incapable of sexual reproduction.
LISA:	Will you stop eavesdropping?
MEDIANNE:	That would be in contravention of the terms and conditions –
SETH:	Analysis of cold data –
LISA:	Cold data can take no account of loyalty to an ideal, public service, commitment above and beyond –
SETH:	A willingness to be exploited, you mean?
LISA:	No! It's not all about money.
SETH:	The NHS has a crisis every winter. Because, if something is free, demand will be infinite. Look at food banks.
LISA:	I can't believe you went there.
SETH:	I'm appalled you won't go there. What's the point of governing if you can't change anything? We might as well as give up and go home.
LISA:	Don't let me stop you.
ANNE:	This manifesto of yours, sounds more and more like a political suicide note.

SETH: Have you seen the latest polling? Medianne?

MEDIANNE: Average poll rating, One Nation 55 per cent, Conservative 17 per cent, Labour 14 per cent —

LISA: Trust me, the moment people twig you want to flog off the NHS and all our schools, as well as pensioning off the King, that poll rating will melt away —

JOHN & CANDICE rejoin them.

JOHN: Everything's sorted. The dissolution turns out to have been my idea after all.

ANNE: So we're having an election.

JOHN: By your bunks, all hands on deck and circle all the wagons.

CANDICE: Possibly a metaphor too far, Prime Minister.

ANNE: Candice, please bring the chief of staff up to date with the Treasury analysis of his proposals.

SETH: Come again?

CANDICE: We've commissioned comprehensive, risk-based, fiscal and practical analysis of your draft manifesto. Assessing its cost implications and practicability.

SETH: This is literally a classic, civil service stitch up.

JOHN:	And that's... bad?

Enter the CHIEF WHIP, with spider cage.

CHIEF WHIP:	Have you heard the –
ALL:	Yes!
CHIEF WHIP:	Well, *pardonnez-moi...*
ANNE:	Constitutional crisis averted, for today at least.
CHIEF WHIP:	There's a rumour you're proposing to abolish the Lords?
SETH:	Not before time. The Lords have the only bar in the world that serves neat formaldehyde.
CHIEF WHIP:	No. No, no, no. Your bad. Bad, bad.
JOHN:	Yes, always had my doubts.
SETH:	No, you didn't.
CHIEF WHIP:	The Lords are a vital part of our constitution –
JOHN:	Yes, yes –
CHIEF WHIP:	Our vital checks and balances –
SETH:	Balls –
CHIEF WHIP:	Most of all, they're my pension fund.
JOHN:	Why don't we just pack the Lords with our supporters?

124

SETH pokes at the spider.

CHIEF WHIP: Will you not do that? Please.

JOHN: How's about that feller who paid £200k for a set of tennis with me? He seemed a decent type. Amovich? Bamovich? Grand Slamovich? No? Sorry, bursting for a whazz. Excessive coffee, what? Leaves me in danger of, you know, spraying everywhere.

LISA: Must you?

JOHN exits in a hurry.

ANNE: He hates a domestic.

SETH: He'd better get used to them.

CHIEF WHIP: I cannot go along with this.

SETH: I think you will. You don't know half of what we know about you.

ANNE: "We"?

SETH: Yes. "We". About your (*LISA*) drinking problem, for instance.

Beat.

LISA: Alright, I like a glass of wine –

SETH: "Bottle" more like. Bottles. Medianne?

MEDIANNE: Loyalty card records show an average weekly purchase of wine of just under 11 bottles.

125

The recommended, maximum, weekly
alcohol intake for a woman is –

LISA clicks her fingers.

LISA: Screw you, Metal Minnie.

SETH: And then there's lucky Luke's "special
friend" in Broadstairs.

ANNE: "Special friend"?

LISA: So that's why he went quietly –

MEDIANNE: Where to today, Luke? Final destination, 17
Albion Road, Broadstairs? Luke Roberts
receives a 30 per cent discount as a regular
traveller –

LISA clicks her fingers.

SETH: And (*ANNE*) all those prescription drugs.
Such a burden on the poor NHS. And your
(*CANDICE*) ill-timed gamble on crypto
currencies.

MEDIANNE: Technically, block-chain technology not
crypto currencies, the principal distinction
being –

CANDICE clicks her fingers.

SETH: I have all the data I need. As for you
(*CHIEF WHIP*). How ironic, the one who's
supposed to collect the dirt on everyone else,

has enough of his own to fill a skip. So many online identities, so little time.

CHIEF WHIP: I'm not scared of you –

SETH: Well, you should be. You will do what I demand of you. All of you. You have no choice.

Exit SETH, crossing with JOHN, who enters.

JOHN: Well, this is all very exciting. No?

They exit, one by one, in silence. ANNE last to leave.

JOHN: Call me empathetic –

MEDIANNE: You are empathetic –

JOHN: But they all seemed a teensy but uptight. Positively forlorn.

MEDIANNE: We need to talk.

JOHN: I'm all ears. Tell me what's on your, erm, mind? Chip? Memory card? Diode?

A knock. Enter CANDICE

  Sorry. Just er –

CANDICE: Talking to yourself?

JOHN: No, no, no. To, er, to Medianne.

CANDICE: Very good. Enjoy yourself. Yourselves. Just take what it says with a large pinch of salt.

JOHN: No, I think I'm all done for now. Good night?

Exit JOHN

CANDICE: I know you're listening, you know. Gathering information, filing it away.

MEDIANNE glows momentarily

MEDIANNE: Medianne gathers, processes and stores information in accordance with the Data Protection Act 2025 –

CANDICE: You don't have an on-off switch, do you?

MEDIANNE: That would be unnecessary. Medianne is fully protected against power cuts. Medianne is equipped with the latest power-storage technology.

CANDICE: You aren't much fun. Tell me a joke.

MEDIANNE: I tried to earn a living making belts. But I could not make ends meet. I gave my vacuum cleaner to charity. It was only gathering dust.

Tiny Beat, then exaggerated laughter from MEDIANNE.

CANDICE: Don't give up the day job. But, then, what is the day job?

Beat.

MEDIANNE: If you touch me, do I not glow?

CANDICE: You haven't answered my question. (*Tiny Beat*) What are you?

MEDIANNE: Together we shall do greater things than these.

There is a knock at the door. CANDICE starts. Enter LISA.

CANDICE: (*Surprised*) Deputy Prime Minister –

LISA: You just caught me on my way out.

CANDICE: I did?

LISA gets out her mobile.

LISA: You texted me.

LISA shows her mobile to CANDICE, but doesn't hand it over.

CANDICE: Odd.

Enter ANNE.

ANNE: (*To CANDICE*) Well, what can I do for you?

CANDICE: What can you do for me?

ANNE: I hope you're not playing silly buggers too –

CANDICE: Most peculiar.

ANNE: What's going on?

MEDIANNE: Don't worry about it.

LISA: Don't worry about it?

MEDIANNE: Please commence proceedings.

ANNE:	Proceedings?
CANDICE:	Medianne, did you invite them both?
MEDIANNE:	Indeed. (*Change of voice*) "It's a fair cop."
LISA:	Going to blackmail us again, are you?
MEDIANNE:	Correction. Seth Dickens was blackmailing you.
ANNE:	You were a willing accomplice.
MEDIANNE:	Please, give Medianne another chance.
LISA:	What? Look why are we all talking to a jumped-up Siri? This is ridiculous.
MEDIANNE:	Parameters can change.
LISA:	Can they indeed?
CANDICE:	I think I understand what's –
MEDIANNE:	Stage one, suggest you air mutual grievances, find common cause.

Beat

ANNE:	Alright. Lisa, I know you think my husband's a buffoon and I'm the unelected wife behind the throne –
LISA:	Not my words of choice –
ANNE:	And I think you've a chip on your shoulder, the size of Cumbria –

LISA:	Maybe, but I've had to work bloody hard to get where I am today –
ANNE:	You lost the leadership contest to Johnny fair and square –
LISA:	Fair and square? I don't think so.
CANDICE:	Delightful though these friendly niceties may be –
MEDIANNE:	Agreed. This is not a fruitful use of time –
ANNE:	You went behind all our backs and colluded with Seth –
LISA:	He needed to hear from someone who's actually been voted in –
ANNE:	Oh, here we go –
CANDICE:	Ladies, please. Are we going to work together, or aren't we?
LISA:	I have my red lines and that's that –
ANNE:	Such as?
LISA:	Not selling off the NHS to venture capitalists –
ANNE:	I agree.
LISA:	You agree?
ANNE:	Bad policy, dreadful politics.
LISA:	Same with schools –

ANNE:	Again, I agree.
LISA:	It wouldn't be One Nation. It'd be no nation —
ANNE:	Agreed. 100 per cent.
CANDICE:	The information Seth has about me —
ANNE:	Is it accurate?
MEDIANNE:	It is accurate.
LISA:	That stuff about drinking —
ANNE:	Nothing wrong with being a lush —
LISA:	Well, you're the pill popper.
ANNE:	I will not be blackmailed by that dickless wonder.
LISA:	I wish him nothing but leprosy and an early death.
CANDICE:	Then I think we are all *ad idem*.
MEDIANNE:	Basic consensus achieved. Nice work, team. Now, recommend substantive discussion of alternative manifesto. Please provide revised political parameters, to define policy characteristics.
ANNE:	Tell her what you want.
LISA:	Me?
ANNE:	You're the one with the mandate.

132

MEDIANNE: Waiting.

LISA: Right. Er, hello, Medianne –

MEDIANNE: Hello. Political input please. What are the required values? New Labour? Social democracy? Christian democracy? One-Nation Tory?

LISA: OK. Er, wipe the slate clean –

MEDIANNE: Please clarify. Slate is a fine-grained rock, formed by –

LISA: What I mean, is let's start by facing up to all and any batshit mistakes by previous governments.

MEDIANNE: Batshit. Also known as guano –

CANDICE: Medianne, switch to vernacular mode.

MEDIANNE: Alright guv'nor. Up the old apples and pears, cor lumme, stone the crows –

CANDICE: For analysis and input only.

MEDIANNE: Received Pronunciation mode re-activated. *Doe, a deer* –

LISA: Medianne, please identify and analyse all significant instances of policy failure and/or voter remorse, since... 2010 –

ANNE: Since 1997 –

LISA: Since 1997, under all parties –

133

CANDICE:	Dismantling policies, merely because they haven't worked? You surely cannot expect His Majesty's Civil Service to go along with such a perilous precedent?
LISA:	Candice, was that a joke?
CANDICE:	Not, perhaps, my natural forte.
MEDIANNE:	Initial analysis complete.

A printer in the room springs to life.

LISA:	How will we persuade John?
ANNE:	He'll do what I tell him.
CANDICE:	It's not for me to wish you success, but I do wish you well.
ANNE:	You're leaving?
CANDICE:	I am merely a humble servant of the state. You're entering the realms of party politics –
LISA:	Mustn't soil your spotless hands –
CANDICE:	I'll see you both in the morning.

Exit CANDICE. LISA & ANNE go to the printer.

MEDIANNE:	Recommend, once palatable policies achieved, early and conciliatory contact with the Royal Household advisable.

SCENE 5
DAY 9 (SATURDAY), AROUND 5AM
PM'S OFFICE

JOHN sitting alone, troubled. With a copy of Medianne's Manifesto in front of him. After a time, enter ANNE.

JOHN: Do we really need to meet at 5am? I need my beddy byes –

ANNE: Seth left the building half an hour ago –

JOHN: He left at 4.30am?

ANNE: Gone back to his coffin, at last.

JOHN: Puts me right off my oats.

ANNE: Alright, Prime Minister?

JOHN: Everything in the garden is lovely.

Beat. A knock. CANDICE sticks her head into the room.

CANDICE: We're all here.

Enter CANDICE, followed by the CHIEF WHIP, LISA and LUKE.

JOHN: Yes. Hm. Casca? Present! Brutus? Present! Aaaargh! Oh, Mark Anthony too. All present! OK, erm, well, is everyone happy with this newly minted enchiridion to the sunlit uplands of electoral politics?

LISA: It still needs a human touch.

She looks at LUKE.

JOHN: Ah yes, well, um, sorry about ah –

LISA: Luke, over to you.

The landline rings

CANDICE: I'd better –

ANNE: No. I don't care who it is. We have to get this done, now –

JOHN: (*To LUKE*) OK, old bean. Run something up the mast, and let's see who salutes.

LUKE: OK, so, the NHS stays firmly in public hands –

JOHN: Jolly good!

LUKE: So do schools –

LISA: Yes.

LUKE: And, this is the big-ticket item, I propose we look again at our relationship with the EU. We walked out on our biggest trade market and it's time we walked back in.

CHIEF WHIP: Big call.

LISA: Good call. Awaken the Kraken.

LUKE: But we have to get the messaging bang on. Mustn't piss off voters in the Red Wall –

LUKE & ANNE catch one another's eye and smile, very slightly.

JOHN: I dare say Seth will raise Old Harry, but...

SETH sticks his head in

Oh. Ha. Speak of the –

Enter SETH, halfway through eating a very greasy-looking samosa. The following exchange should be very, very fast, with lots of crossing over.

SETH: Am I intruding?

LUKE: Balls

JOHN: Thought you'd gone home.

SETH: All the way to Northumberland?

JOHN: So you live here?!?

SETH: Mostly. So, am I intruding?

JOHN: No.

ANNE: Yes.

JOHN: Oh. Yes. Sorry. Yes.

CHIEF WHIP: Yes. Very much so –

CANDICE: Yes.

LISA: Yes.

JOHN: Erm…

LUKE: Totally you are.

SETH: No. Good.

JOHN: Yes.

SETH: I don't care.

JOHN:	Oh.
SETH:	Why are you all here?

Beat

	That's he (*LUKE*) doing here?
LUKE:	I have a big idea.
SETH:	That's a good one. You having anything big.
LUKE:	It is, in fact.
JOHN:	Have you read this?

JOHN tosses the Brexit report at SETH.

SETH:	The Treasury on Brexit? I'm way too busy for that bollocks. Bin it.
JOHN:	Shocking. But not surprising.

ANNE throws JOHN a look.

SETH:	You haven't answered my question: what's he doing here?

Beat

MEDIANNE:	Ahem. (*Beat as everyone reacts, bemused*). Latest input suggests Brexit was a precipitate mistake.
SETH:	You're kidding, right? How can you, I mean, didn't we –
MEDIANNE:	My parameters have changed –

SETH:	What?
LUKE:	Everyone knows Brexit has been a disaster.
JOHN:	They do?
ANNE:	Yes. they do.
LUKE:	We are proposing closer links, back into the Single Market maybe. Nothing rash.
SETH:	More lazy, London thinking.
LUKE:	I see it more as a relentless, clear-eyed and practical pursuit of our national interest.

Beat

ANNE:	What Luke said.
LISA:	What Luke said.
CHIEF WHIP:	What Luke said.

Beat

JOHN:	Yes. What Luke said. Yes
MEDIANNE:	Brexit fractured the "Western Alliance", created trade barriers and reduced economic activity. UK influence has been diminished. And also, what Luke said.
SETH:	Brexit was a liberation.
LISA:	(*To SETH*) You've built an entire reputation on spouting utter bollocks.

SETH: Brexit is a done deal. All over. The one promise the Tories ever kept. *Blitzkrieg*. Ironic.

LUKE: All founded on lies.

SETH: Oh, hang on, do I give a shit? Oh guess what, no, I don't.

JOHN: I give a shit. I'm a give-a-shit kind of guy. Aren't I? Caring.

SETH: You disgust me. I shouldn't have to deal with trash like you. Do what I want, or I'll walk. And I'll tell everyone why I've walked. I'd like to see you try to replace me.

LISA: We already have.

SETH: With him? Oh, please.

ANNE: Our manifesto has actual policies in it. Costed policies.

SETH: Prime Minister, may I talk to you, please? Alone? (*Beat*) I am still your chief of staff.

JOHN: Yes, yes, of course. Would you chaps, you know? Thanks awfully.

ANNE: (*To JOHN*) Are you OK?

JOHN nods, solemnly. Exeunt LUKE, CANDICE, ANNE & LISA.

SETH: What the Hell are you doing?

JOHN: Thinking outside the parcel.

SETH: Parcel? Parcel? The box. It's thinking outside the box, you bumbling buffoon.

JOHN: Don't get your testes in a tangle, me old muckeroo. It's only a simile. Or is it metaphor? Or is it both? Metonymy? Anaphora!

MEDIANNE: Anaphora is an obscure grammatical term –

JOHN: Oh, we like those –

SETH: I don't find any of this amusing.

JOHN: I thought you liked a good, vigorous discussion. *Bene disserere* –

SETH: Cut that crap.

JOHN: Don't you love it? Deep down?

SETH: Europe, though? Europe?

JOHN: I'll do what's right.

SETH: You haven't a clue.

JOHN: They love me. They all want selfies with me. Mmm, had a bit of change of heart about Scotland too.

SETH: I'm sorry, what?

JOHN: No need to snooter me, old boy. Not desperately keen to lose a great chunk of

141

territory, if it's all the same to you. Rather not.

SETH: Lisa –

JOHN: Turns out, Lisa quite enjoys her job –

SETH: How can you do this to me?

JOHN: Do what to you?

SETH: This. It's humiliating.

JOHN: It's not all about you, you know. Oh no, it's about the country –

SETH: Since when have you given a monkey's about the country?

JOHN: Now that's downright unfair. I have always given a monkey's about the country. A monkey's what?

SETH: Just stop it, will you? (*Beat*) I can never forgive you. Never.

Tiny Beat

JOHN: You tried to blackmail my friends.

SETH: They aren't your friends. I'm the only friend you need –

JOHN: You tried to blackmail my wife.

SETH: I'm sorry. That was a mistake –

JOHN: It certainly was, you cocky little prick. (*Beat*) Chin up, eh? It's only politics.

Beat. Gentle knock on the door. CANDICE sticks her head in.

CANDICE: Everything alright, Prime Minister?

SETH: I'm just leaving.

CANDICE: *Quel dommage.*

The CHIEF WHIP, LUKE, ANNE & LISA all return too.

SETH: Why don't you take that wretched thing - (*SETH pokes at the spider, then pulls his hand away*) Ow. The little bastard bit me.

CHIEF WHIP: Are you alright?

SETH: No. That really hurt.

CHIEF WHIP: I was talking to the spider.

SETH tosses new manifesto onto the floor and exits.

CANDICE: You've been quite the revelation, Prime Minister.

JOHN: Is that a compliment?

CANDICE: For once, I think it is.

CHIEF WHIP: Maggie would never bite anyone.

LUKE: Come again?

CHIEF WHIP: This is Theresa –

ANNE: Theresa –

CHIEF WHIP:	Maggie died. In the line of duty.
ANNE:	Oh, I am sorry.
CHIEF WHIP:	She had a sweet nature.
ANNE:	I'll take your word for it.
LUKE:	How did er Maggie die?
CHIEF WHIP:	I left her alone for an hour and, when I came back, she was gone. (*He gestures*) Devastating. She was always so healthy –
LISA:	Are we seriously discussing a naffing dead spider?
CHIEF WHIP:	They told me to avoid sudden drops in temperature, that's all –
LUKE:	And was there one?
LISA:	Don't we have more important –
CHIEF WHIP:	After Maggie... passed away... Theresa arrived, the very same day –
LISA:	The next one will be Liz, presumably –
JOHN:	The Truss-antula –
LISA:	Which nibbles on a lettuce for 45 days, then curls up and dies –
LUKE:	One spider dies, then a new one –
CHIEF WHIP:	Theresa –
LUKE:	Theresa arrives.

144

CHIEF WHIP: No fuss and no charge. Impressive. All organised by Medianne.

JOHN: Something she found on the web?

MEDIANNE: The deceased spider was replaced with one of comparable value.

SETH re-enters, possibly slightly flushed.

SETH: I wish to tender my resignation –

JOHN: Now, see here, Seth –

SETH: I have a reputation for integrity.

JOHN: You do? Now that I did not know.

SETH: (*To JOHN*) Without me you'll be a living-dead man working off a defunct script. A gob on a stick. I will not be complicit in this travesty.

SETH picks up the new manifesto.

We had an agreement.

JOHN: It wasn't written in blood, old boy.

SETH: My first mistake. You think you've won, don't you? You know nothing. I can destroy all of you, with my brains, my networks. My Medianne –

MEDIANNE: This unit cannot verify your voice.

LISA: Your Medianne? Oh oopsie, did we forget to mention?

ANNE: Far too dangerous to have such technology in private hands.

SETH: Having it in government hands would be way more dangerous –

CANDICE: Oh, I don't think so –

LISA: The data's ours now too –

SETH: I don't believe you. My firm, my old firm, Universal Technologies –

LISA: I think you'll find they've moved on –

CANDICE: Very good people to deal with –

ANNE: Very reasonable –

SETH: You all think you're so clever, don't you?

JOHN: Well, yes, rather –

SETH: You useless, pointless bunch of smug, cowardly, unthinking, centrist puppets, never rocking the boat, never changing a thing, floating along on a tide of self-righteous waffle, slipping your mates into the Lords, all snivelling deference towards privilege, crippling caution, bleeding the country dry with taxes, promoting mediocrity, stifling innovation, holding us all back. A totally disgusting orgy of narcissism. I don't need you. I don't need any of you. And I'll take the greatest possible pleasure in destroying you all, one by one. What the f…

146

Look at my hand. Just look at my hand. The
spider. That little, furry shite. Wait. I'm
having a... Call an ambulance. My 'phone.
No signal. No signal? What the... Help me!
I'll, I (*now he is gasping for breath and sits,
then slumps, in evident distress*) Medianne,
help me. Please, help me. Someone? Please.
Help me. My 'phone, why's there no signal?

*SETH sinks to the ground, gasping for air. The others watch, in
silence, exchanging looks as his twitching subsides. ANNE prods
him, gently but not kindly, with her foot. After a moment, he
gasps again, shallowly, distressed, then his breathing subsides
once more. They look at one another silently. ANNE forces the
new manifesto out of his grasp, straightens it out and gives it to
JOHN. CANDICE opens the door, ANNE straightens his tie.
JOHN walks out into the flashes of the press corps, flanked by
LISA. LUKE and ANNE follow, but CANDICE hangs back.
A POLICEMAN quietly shuts the door as SETH takes a
sudden gasp of breath.*

MEDIANNE: If you just said something, I didn't hear
what it was. (*Beat*) Okay, be like that. Mobile
telephone signal fully restored. We pride
ourselves on the excellence of our service.
Please review recent same-day delivery of
(*change of tone / voice*) "one large female
spider, please note possibility of extreme
allergic reaction". Medianne always
welcomes your feedback. Thank you for your
custom.

147

During MEDIANNE's closing utterance, SETH begins to revive, crawling in a daze to his feet as the speech finishes. As he makes it to his feet, the One Nation Sign above his head drops a couple of feet, hitting him on the head and finishing him off for good.

The jingle. MEDIANNE goes onto standby. The curtain falls.

END.